I0438828

'ABCs' of Emotions:
Help Inside

'ABCs' of Emotions: Help Inside

By

Howard V. Otterholt, Ph.D.

Copyright © 1999 by Howard V. Otterholt

All rights reserved. No part of this book may be reproduced,
stored in a retrieval system, or transmitted by any means,
electronic, mechanical, photocopying, recording, or otherwise,
without written permission from the author.

ISBN 1-58721-084-3

1stBooks – rev. 02/25/00

About The Book

This book is for parents, teachers, preachers, serious students, and anyone having family problems.

Negativity causes stress. Stress kills slowly but as surely as with a gun. Negativity from childhood becomes manifest in adult negative desires, beliefs, and emotions that drive and inhibit behavior and affect decision-making. It affects mind, body, and spirit.

Understanding of the childhood development of emotionally driven and emotionally inhibited behavior leads to understanding and forgiveness of offenders, past, present, and future. This results in reduction of anger, frustration, and helplessness. It builds confidence and self-esteem. Forgiveness, along with acceptance of the randomness of circumstance, is essential for physical, emotional, and spiritual health.

This book will help the reader to build and strengthen an understanding of the beginnings of desires, beliefs, and emotions, and of emotionally driven and emotionally inhibited behavior. With believed understanding, forgiveness is automatic. The expected results are positive changes in emotions, and in life and living. Many hundreds in therapy have learned, understood and believed what is presented herein. Their lives changed significantly for the better, some dramatically.

Are you feeling
Down?
Anxiety?
Anger?
Low self-esteem?
Helpless?
Stressed?
Pressured at Work?
Manipulated?
Abandoned?
Abused?

Are you having
Relationship Problems?
Family Problems?

Are you a
Parent?
Teacher?
Preacher?
Serious student?
Counselor?
or
Therapist?

HELP INSIDE!

Other than for fair use, and for the use of Appendices for making self-help tapes, or for formatting a decision paper for personal use, or for composing a letter to your child caretakers, this book, or any part of it, may not in any form or method be reproduced, stored for retrieval, or transmitted without prior written consent of the Otterholt Family Trust

Important Message to Readers

This book contains material for informational and educational purposes only. It is not a substitute for professional care of any type. Anyone with any type of physical or psychological illness or problem should consult a physician or other health care professional. It is the responsibility of the reader to consult with his or her own healthcare professional to determine the appropriateness of using data found in this book, including the self-help audio tapes as referenced and described in the Appendices.

DEDICATION

This book is dedicated to my wife, Iola,

and our five children, Ann, Janet,

James, Connie, and Susan.

I would like to thank my wife for her patience while I fumbled with two keyboards and while editing the text, over and over.

Next, I express regrets to our children, now adults, for my ignorance and lack of understanding of them when they were very young. I had not yet learned.

Table of Contents

Chapter 1
A PREVIEW

Introduction

I forgive easily because I know that the behavior of those who have offended me was and is not consciously controlled. WHAT?!? WHOA!! *That can't* be true! – Can it? ---- It *can be*, and it *is*. For now, consider that it just might be, and read on.

IMAGINE. I am walking down the street in an old and very rough residential area of a large city. Poorly maintained apartment buildings, dirty windows, a naked child, tipped trash cans and litter in every direction. As I walk, I cannot help but look and wonder. I bump into a man. We both quickly say, "Excuse me." I continue walking and gawking. I bump into another man. Before I can apologize he calls me stupid, tells me to watch where I'm going, and walks away. Again I proceed curiously down the street. I bump into a big man. Before I can say a word, he strikes out with his fist. In pain I continue walking and looking. I must be a slow learner. As I am looking around once more, I bump into a man who quickly pulls a gun and BANG-BANG I'm dead.

Four personalities. Why? All perhaps raised in the same neighborhood. Four sets of beliefs. Four sets of desires. Four sets of emotions. Four different impulsive reactions. Why?

If an adult's childhood experiences were predominantly happy, if he was treated with respect, received demonstrated love, and was taught and trained in moral values, he is likely emotionally and physically healthy. He feels good, looks forward to work each day, and enjoys meeting old friends and making new ones. He is optimistic about the future, and demonstrates a sense of propriety. His behavior is generally acceptable to society.

Conversely, early ridicule, abuse, and over-control or neglect have negative effects on a child and later on the adult. The negative effects are physical, emotional, spiritual, and behavioral. Later as an adult he may feel stressed, frustrated, angry, helpless, rejected, and perhaps anti-social. Society often does not deem his behavior acceptable and may react in ways that are very hurtful to him. His emotions and behavior worsen.

One may find himself in a position of wanting to do something and at the same time not wanting to do it. Recall of fearful memories of believed consequences may inhibit an otherwise emotionally driven and risky or immoral behavior. Recall of memories of strong moral beliefs, and feeling good about them, inhibits one type of behavior and drives another. One's ultimate decision, though not necessarily moral, is the one about which he feels the best at the moment. It is the unconscious desires and emotions associated with those beliefs that drive and inhibit behavior. They affect behavior in family and social life, school, the workplace, and personal relationships. They bias decisions.

Because of them, one acts, reacts, overreacts, or is *inhibited* from acting. They affect decisions of self and everyone else - of friends, employers, teachers, preachers, and presidents. Positive beliefs and feelings contribute to positive living. Negative beliefs and feelings reduce the ability to perceive accurately, to analyze, and to make sound, moral decisions. Overcoming them requires understanding, forgiveness, and acceptance of circumstance. The payback is in feeling better regardless of how one now feels.

Everyone has degrees of emotional ups and downs. At any given time a person may feel wonderful. An hour later, in a different environment, he may feel even better, or he may feel anxious, angry, distraught, depressed, or only uncomfortable. Much of what he is feeling is the result of sensing something similar to what has been sensed and felt earlier. Through unconscious association, what is being sensed now is linked to and may recall desires, feelings, and beliefs experienced in the past. Linkages begin to form during infancy They may well be called psychotrails, psychowebs, or intranets.

Appropriate reading and learning may trigger positive changes in one's life irrespective of who, what, and how he is, and how good he feels. He may view young and old with a new dimension of interest, and may be better enabled to help those about whom he cares.

For more than 27 years it has been my privilege to have worked in therapy with hundreds of troubled clients from 16 States, the District of Columbia, and 14 other countries. They recalled and reassessed early experiences. They found and understood truths that were new to them. They accepted the unfairness of circumstance, and forgave offenders, past and present. They changed their lives, often dramatically.

A second privilege is that of currently working voluntarily with prison inmates who are having problems with frustration, anger, rage, low self-esteem, and helplessness, even hopelessness. The benefit of forgiveness can be seen in the change in demeanor and facial expression of an angry and hopeless inmate who comes to understand and forgive.

To know and believe that forgiveness is real, it is critical that the forgiver understand and believe that behavior is not consciously controlled, but that it is driven and inhibited by associative recall of childhood-initiated desires, beliefs, and emotions. They began when everyone else was in control. Understanding this promotes forgiveness. The benefits of *felt* forgiveness are almost indescribable.

A television minister, Dr. Robert Schuller said, "I am not free until I believe in me." New positive beliefs build self-esteem. They help one believe in himself. They help him avoid stressing himself both emotionally and physically. With reading he can come to understand how he and others became what they are, why they feel, believe, and behave as they do, and how they can effect change, *if they desire.*

This book is a manifest effort to help readers reach a higher level understanding of what is necessary to really forgive, to be able to do so, to overcome negative beliefs and desires, and to accept the randomness of circumstance. Forgiving may require changes in beliefs. If one resists change, he limits himself to what he already knows, believes, understands, and can do. Forgiveness is not the very wrong "forgive and forget" of the uninformed. It is instead, the critically important "*remember without the hurt.*"

The Appendices contain step-by-step instructions and suggested affirmations for making your own self-help audio tapes. Their purposes are to help the listener to relax, reduce anxiety, build self-esteem, stop smoking, promote healing, say no-to-cancer, and control eating habits.

You will encounter repetition for a reason you will come to understand. You will read a lot about negativity. That is wherein lie the problems that need resolution. You will find split infinitives for better emphasis. You will find sentences that end in prepositions, but understanding is what is important. There is an old tale told by grammarians about a little boy ill in his upstairs bedroom. His mother took a book upstairs and sat down by his bed. Her son asked, "Mom, why did you bring that book I didn't want to be read to out of up for?" Ending in *five* prepositions, but easily understood.

The remainder of this chapter contains abstracts, by chapter, that tell you what I am going to tell you about reduction of anxiety and stress through understanding of self and others, and the resolution of other negativity including anger and low self-esteem.

Preview Chapter 2. The Unconscious Mind

An *experience* is remembered as an event, the memory of which is linked with memories of associated unfulfilled desires, physical feelings, emotions felt at the time, whatever is perceptually sensed by any of the five senses, and whatever is believed or concluded during the event. Whew!

Since infancy, memories of significant experiences have been stored in the subconscious or unconscious mind. If an experience is significant, the memory of its associatively linked aspects will reach unconscious long-term memory. Feeling or remembering one aspect may recall any or all of the others. Of all the aspects of past experiences, it is one's *feelings or emotions*, whether painful or joyful, that are most commonly recalled, and generally without awareness as to the origin.

Each feeling has an infinite number of levels. After infancy, no feeling is felt alone. Each is combined and felt with other feelings. What is felt is a *composite* of feelings, an *emotion*. Because degrees of complexity in the unconscious are infinite,

4

one can never completely know another person.

Emotions associated with a childhood experience may be so painful as to test the limits of adult tolerance. Memory of the traumatic event and its associated and fully felt emotions may be repressed beyond conscious recall. However, *to a degree,* the *emotions* may be recalled. They will drive and inhibit behavior, sometimes in an instant. The resulting behavior may be violence, compulsive sexual acts, or any of a host of other negative reactions. Conversely, the results of happy childhood experiences may result in adult enthusiasm, acts of kindness, a healthy sense of humor, and gregariousness.

The intranet of linkages between and among associated memories is analogous to the entangled vines in a dense jungle. Tugging on one vine may shake only one other vine even though it is indirectly connected to all. Tugging on two vines may shake many of them. Because of the complex intertwining, strong and persistent tugging on three or four vines may drag up one or more of the buried roots of those vines and of several others.

Similarly, if at a given time, one is aware of sensing only one aspect of the environment, such as tasting a disliked food, he may associatively recall a composite of merely unpleasant feelings. Tasting the same type of food while also listening to a once familiar but disliked musical number may precipitate a composite of even more feelings. The emotion felt is stronger and more complicated. Still later while in a restaurant, multiple reminders of tasting the same type of food, listening to the same music, *plus* watching and hearing a loud argument at a nearby table may recall associated root causes, the beginnings of the negative emotions being currently experienced. The emotions will be felt more strongly because of encountering more simultaneous reminders of more negative feelings felt during more past negative experiences.

Preview Chapter 3. Effects of the Unconscious

One may feel healthy, happy, and optimistic, or he may feel frustrated, angry, unloved, and helpless. He may blame others. Emotions may be felt without a clue as to why, or as to its short and long-range effect on mind and body. For good or bad, they affect behavior, which in turn affects interpersonal relationships in school, at home, in the workplace, and in social life. Emotions and beliefs may rise almost simultaneously as if multiplexed. They cause action, overreaction, procrastination, inhibition, or outright prevention.

The Apostle, Paul, wrote that he did what he hated and could not find a way to do what he wanted to do. His letter to the Romans gives examples of his inner conflicts. (Romans 7:15-23) No one is completely free of them.

Some of one's beliefs may be in conflict with those of most of society. Some may be in conflict with other beliefs within his *own* belief system. This is commonly known as inner conflict. Each belief rises and falls. The belief that is stronger at the moment is the one that biases decision- making. It has risen to a strong degree because of better feelings *about* that belief. The belief and feelings are at work up to the very moment of implementing the decision. With even minor changes in the perceived environment, a conflicting belief may strengthen. Regrets may set in. Rapid swings are manifest in indecision. No one is totally free of inner conflict. No one is totally free of bias. One person may believe a race of people to be superior. Another may believe in a woman's right to abortion. Another may believe in God. Each may have doubts or inner conflicts regarding his own beliefs.

Equally intelligent people profess divergent or opposing beliefs. Which is correct? Democrat, Republican, third party, or none? Brown or white eggs? Red or brown potatoes? Imported or domestic autos? And on and on. "I know I'm right."

Social anxiety affects millions. It ranges from mere shyness to severe agoraphobia which can reach a stage of panic fear of leaving home. It often stems from a child's earlier expectations of criticism and ridicule by anyone he encounters.

Two very significant aspects of one's environment are another's behavior and words directed toward him. One may hear a compliment or a putdown. One may see and misperceive an expression on another's face. Because of his biases he may misunderstand another's intent without any awareness of the biases.

Environments are ever changing. One senses sights, sounds, odors, tastes, and physical contacts. Sensing aspects of one's current environment serves as a reminder to the unconscious mind of past experiences during which similar environmental aspects were sensed. *Accurate perception* of the aspects of one's current environment may recall memories of joyous feelings. The memories will be *felt. Misperception* of the same aspects will recall *different* memories. They may be of anger, helplessness, even hopelessness. Even though the emotions are now strongly felt, memories of the causative *events* may not come into awareness.

When one interacts with others, or merely *thinks* of doing so, feelings from the past are associatively recalled. They drive and inhibit behavior without one's knowing why.

Preview Chapter 4. Early Childhood

During infancy, words are heard, events observed, and physical pain felt. None of this as yet has any meaning to the infant. However, *memories* of what is seen, of what is physically felt, and of hearing words spoken loudly, emotionally, or repeatedly are stored in unconscious long-term memory. Later as the child matures he learns the meanings of what he had sensed during earlier experiences. Memories of newly learned knowledge are stored and linked with the previously stored memories of those words which, when first heard, were not understood. They are also linked with memories of perceptions of the earlier *events*. Memories of events are not as readily recalled as are memories of emotions.

Depending on what he had heard even while in his mother's womb, and how he was subsequently treated, he may feel unwanted, unloved, angry, inadequate, or he may feel happy, confident, and enthused. He now unconsciously *believes* the once meaningless words, phrases, and sentences. He has developed beliefs about what he had seen, heard, and physically felt, but not then understood. Later, emotions rise *without* any conscious awareness of having heard and experienced the earlier associated events.

Everyone has learned and stored in the unconscious mind at least some misperceived and unreasoned "truths" from childhood. Family life is expected to be a source of feelings of trust, security, and confidence, but even the best of parenting is not always perceived as such by a child.

A child is offended when he misperceives loving care, in the form of parental love and control, as offensive. "Mom never lets me swim in the river, but *I* don't think it's too dirty. *I* don't think it would make me sick just because a couple of other kids got sick. Joey's mom lets *him* do it. His mom sure must love him. I guess mine doesn't love me. She won't even let me play in the street, not ever. I could dodge those cars. It makes me mad. Mom just doesn't understand. It makes me mad." Future similar misperceived loving care will reinforce the negative beliefs and emotions.

IMAGINE. Four-year-old Kathy has a loving and caring mother. Today is Kathy's birthday. Her mom had a party for her. Kathy received a new game. She wants her mother to play the game with her. Mom promises her she will play as soon as she finishes cleaning the kitchen. Kathy patiently sits in the kitchen doorway in her new little chair, a present from Mom. She sees Mom finally putting the cleaning equipment away and washing her hands. "Now she's through. Now she'll play with me." The phone rings. It is a very good friend back from a long trip. Mom momentarily interrupts her conversation and tells Kathy, "Sweetheart, play with your dolls. We'll play the game after I get off the phone." She resumes her phone conversation. They continue talking for a long time. Kathy feels rejected and momentarily unloved. "Mom did not tell me the truth. I guess I'm not important to her. That person on the phone is more important. Mom is supposed to love me but she didn't keep her promise. She lied."

Further similar experiences will reinforce her belief that those who are supposed to *love* her will *lie* to her and break their promises. Now she learns about God. She is told that God loves her. She learns of God's promises. Her unconscious mind, her belief system, contains a "Yes, but..." Her unconscious contains her *own* truths about love and promises.

If a child misbehaves, the parent may feel a childlike desire of wanting to hit back, a need for recognition, or a need to feel superior, or at least equal. A parent may be too preoccupied to devote time to the child. A parent's priorities may be very different from what is needed for and wanted by the child. The child is offended. If this type of treatment is repetitious, the child develops low self-esteem and feelings of wanting revenge and of unfairness and anger, even at God. He misbehaves, perhaps violently. The biblical sins of the fathers have now become manifest in the child.

Preview Chapter 5. Parenting and the Family System

Within the family system, each member's behavior affects directly or indirectly every other member now and into the future. Each family member is a part of every other member's external environment. Parents may believe that their children should have similar behavior, yet one son is gregarious, enjoys meeting and talking with anyone and everyone while his brother sits unhappily and silently in the corner of a room in which several other children are happily playing together. Each child has different perceptions and beliefs, different environments. Each develops a different set of desires, beliefs, and emotions, and in different degrees. Each child's behavior has an effect on siblings. As a result, children in the same family may demonstrate a wide variety of behaviors.

Family life provides the major environment in a child's life. It serves as a basis for development and later recall of moral values and beliefs, and of feelings of love, confidence, and just plain happiness, *or otherwise*. It is the primary environment in which the development of emotions, desires, and beliefs is directed, and accelerated or decelerated. It has been said that a teenager's brain is work-in-progress, however the same may be said of a preteener, a toddler, or an 80-year-old who continues to learn.

If parents do not begin training a child when he is very young, development of parts of the brain is deferred. Some neuroscientists believe in the adage, *use it or lose it*. In a young child, it is likely, *use it or it will not develop in a timely manner*.

If a preteener is not counseled, taught, and trained in values and reasoning needed by a teenager, the teenager's brain is not ready to deal with teenage issues. He will not be able to perceive accurately, reason in an unbiased manner, and reach a moral conclusion. He will not have the *confidence* to take a stand on morality. If parents do not accept their rightful responsibility, the child *will* be taught, trained, and conditioned by *someone, somehow*, but by whom, how, and *in what*?

With parental understanding and timely training, the development of negativity in a child can be constrained. Teaching and training must be moral, caring, and *sustained*. To be effective, training must include persistent but reasonable control, disciplinary action, age-appropriate latitude, and sustained and repeated demonstrations of love, respect, and moral values.

Preview Chapter 6. Family Violence

Physical, sexual, or emotional abuse stresses everyone in the family. It affects physical and mental health now and far into the future. Violence or incest devastates a family. A battered wife may remain in her situation because of complex emotions including fear and dependency.

An abused elderly person feeling helpless, dependent, and fearful is unlikely to report the abuse. A child abused by a parent has such a powerful need for love that he likely will not tell anyone of the abuse because of fear of losing or never receiving that love. He feels both love and rage toward an abusive parent.

A child, spouse, or elderly person may be abused physically, sexually, or emotionally, even *abandoned*. If you have experienced *any* of this, or even *suspect* that you have, PLEASE CONTINUE READING THIS BOOK – CAREFULLY - STUDIOUSLY! I repeat, only through believed understanding and forgiveness can the resulting negative desires, beliefs, and emotions be resolved.

Preview Chapter 7. Understand, Forgive, and Love

One who is offended may feel and retain feelings of anger or resentment, perhaps rage, and may never want to let go of them. These emotions stress the body, interfere with reasoning, and may even briefly arrest thinking. They cause physical illness, and shorten life. Forgiveness will reduce stress. It is a rare person, if any, that is not carrying at least some unconscious envy, contempt, resentment or anger toward someone, perhaps without knowing why and perhaps from as far back as the toddler stage.

Many believe that forgiveness of offenders is warranted, but may only *speak* words of forgiveness. Sadly, many who articulate forgiveness do not feel it. They may *speak* the words, but only to meet others' expectations. *Understanding* is the path to feeling forgiveness. This is a giant step beyond merely *speaking* the words, which may be no forgiveness at all.

For several hours yesterday I met with a group of prison inmates. One had attended only two previous sessions. He is a Christian and an avid reader of the Bible. He *said* he had forgiven *everyone*. He disclosed that he had been a battered child. He said his mother had not just whipped him but had *flogged* him often and without giving reasons.

As he spoke of her his fists tightened, his face became flushed, and his arms jerked forward as though he were going to strike out. He was in a state of rage. His words of forgiveness, without a believed understanding of his mother's emotionally driven behavior, had been futile.

After a time-out to let him cool down, I again explained and reminded him of emotionally driven and inhibited behavior. He eventually agreed that he understood. I asked him to close his eyes and imagine that he was hugging her. He resisted but after further explanation he agreed to do so.

After a few moments he smiled and said he could feel her love. I had never before seen him appear other than sad or angry. I requested that he speak the words to her, "I understand." He opened his eyes and said he *did not understand* how she could have beaten him so often. I reminded him that he had been carrying *his* emotions around since *childhood*. He agreed that it affected his behavior. I reminded him that the *same* was true of his mother and again asked him to close his eyes and imagine he was hugging her. I requested that he now speak out loud, "Mom, I understand and I forgive you."

He spoke the words. After a few moments, he smiled. His smile grew wider. He said, "I feel different." He opened his eyes and tapped his chest and exclaimed, "Whooo-eee!! I feel lighter. I got rid of a heavy load of something. I don't know what. Thank you. Thank you. I don't have to carry that around anymore. *I know I love my Mom and she loves me.*" I explained that I had done nothing, and that it was he who had helped himself.

Forgiveness is a critical step in acquiring and maintaining physical, emotional, and spiritual health. Merely *speaking* words of forgiveness is not enough. A conscious desire to forgive is only the beginning. Forgiveness is genuine only through unconsciously believed understanding of the whys of emotionally driven and emotionally inhibited behavior of offenders. It does not imply approval, nor does it imply one's willingness to tolerate.

With unconsciously believed understanding, forgiveness occurs automatically. It can be felt even while being subjected to offensive behavior. With understanding, new anger does not rise and new negative emotions do not build up. Growth in the ability to forgive is accelerated by understanding the problems of children, of the family system, of interpersonal relationships, the workplace, and of the criminals in our midst. The forgiver will know that his forgiveness is real when he can remember the offender and the offense *without feeling any negative emotions*.

Preview Chapter 8. Feeling and Being Better

Along with understanding and forgiveness, a further contribution to health is the acceptance of the randomness of circumstance, making the best of it with what one has, and getting on with living. From birth and before, all are victims and beneficiaries of circumstance. This is often referred to as luck, good or bad; being born in the USA or not; living on a high and solid hill during a flood, or not; living in tornado alley and having a twister jump clear of your home, or not; having a home survive an earthquake undamaged, or not. Circumstance may result in feelings of happiness and joy, or it may be a source of negativity and stress.

A very young child's life from dawn to dawn is circumstantial to him. Others are in control. It is imposed on every child by bigger and older others, often unintentionally. It may also be imposed by random encounters with strangers, or by random so-called acts-of-God.

The young can rarely accept the unfairness of negative circumstance as being circumstantial. At times, every young child feels and *is trapped* in his world of circumstance. Adults are in charge and may knowingly, or unintentionally and out of ignorance, mistreat the young who cannot understand the whys.

Feelings of frustration and self-pity carry into adulthood. Reduction of frustration and stress requires acceptance of negative circumstance without the thoughts of "Poor me - why *me*?" The benefit of lamenting or commiserating over bad luck is less than zero. It tends to alienate family members, friends, co-workers, and acquaintances.

Two persons may have similar negative emotions or problems. One may recognize the problem, does not want to live that way any more, and takes action to resolve it. The other may believe that help is not needed, or not available. He may express, "He's the one that has the problem, not I," or "I already know all that. It won't do me any good just because it helped them. I'll never get better."

But he *can* get better! When he recognizes the problem, when he has had enough, he does something about it. He *can* change. If he has made himself *ill*, he can make himself *well*. If he already feels well, he can feel *better*. He can sustain good feelings longer.

Preview Chapter 9. Surviving the Workplace

The workplace stresses employees, managers, executives, and indirectly their loved ones, friends, and even acquaintances.

Stress is self-imposed. An employee may fear termination from his job, but often for imagined reasons. Managers may be stressed by incompetence in themselves or subordinates, and by uncooperative employees. Some live in fear. Managers and executives have a longer way to fall. There is clearly a need for understanding and forgiveness in the workplace.

Good employee and management practices, coupled with understanding, will significantly reduce feelings of frustration, helplessness, and of being trapped in a job while at the same time fearing loss of it. Understanding problems in the workplace and knowing and recognizing good management practices will assist in deciding whether to leave or stay. With understanding, feelings of envy, fear, resentment, and anger toward peers, subordinates, and "superiors" will dramatically reduce or even disappear. The workplace will then no longer be deemed a stress-place for those who understand, and for those about whom they care, or for those whom they encounter outside the home and workplace.

Preview Chapter 10. The Closet of the Mind

Therapy abstracts serve as evidence of the cause and effect of negative desires, beliefs, and emotions. They also reveal the positive results of finding the early truths, and of understanding and forgiving offenders and accepting circumstance.

Negativity from the past is recalled and felt here and now. Fortunately, while in a deep state of relaxation one can follow a path back to the source. Because of the deep state of relaxation, and as evidenced in the abstracts, those in hypnotherapy were able to do so. Almost without exception, they were able to articulate their memories of childhood and of later reinforcing experiences that led to adult pathological desires, beliefs, emotions, and ensuing behavior. They came to understand and believe the causes of their problems. After coming to understand themselves and those who had offended them, and after acceptance of circumstance, they could remember the offenses without the previously felt negative emotions. New and healthy beliefs overwhelmed the old negative beliefs. As a result, behavior was modified.

Each person has his own biases, i.e., his own dominant truths, right or wrong, moral or immoral, that affect perception, behavior, and reasoning. Because of unconscious conflicting beliefs, one may persist in denying truths even in the face of undeniable evidence.

Preview Chapter 11. Crime and Consequences

Crime affects everyone. It stresses everyone directly or indirectly. Irrespective of precautions in the home, during travel, at work, while shopping, or attending public or private functions, no one can feel 100% safe. No one can feel his property is immune. Some crimes are termed victimless, but *are* they? Someone will be stressed. It may be the criminal's loved ones. A potential criminal's behavior is controlled only by his belief in moral values, or by his belief of the probability of negative consequences. Parents primarily and other adults must bring the young to believe in moral values, but also that the punishment will fit the crime.

Various levels of government have not been able to build jails and prisons fast enough. The costs of incarcerating criminals have risen to an unreasonable level. They will continue and likely increase at a faster rate unless and until the public decides it has had enough. Permissiveness must stop if crime is to be reduced. Costs of incarceration can be significantly reduced. Inmates can be put to work. Voters can come to understand *their* role in all of this.

Preview Chapter 12. Once More for the Road

With forgiveness, and with acceptance of the randomness and uncontrollability of circumstance as being random and uncontrollable, positive changes in one's life will immediately be realized. Believed understanding of unconsciously driven and inhibited behavior is critical to the ability to forgive. You will read it in different contexts. My hope is that you will come to believe it. You will read it every way I know how to state it.

Repetition promotes unconscious belief.

Understanding reduces stress and anxiety. Emotional, physical, and spiritual health improve. Barring circumstance, you will likely live longer and feel better while doing so. You *do* have a degree of control over *exposure* to many of your circumstances.

Nothing in this book is intended to interfere with any past, current, intended, referred, needed, or considered advice, care, or treatment from any physician, minister, health care professional, or any other generally recognized valid source of treatment, counseling, or therapeutics.

Chapter 2
THE UNCONSCIOUS

The Belief System

One makes countless decisions every day, most of them automatic and not stressful. Look to the right, look left, sit, stand, pick up tooth brush, apply tooth paste, brush, rinse, undress, get into bed, arrange covers, move pillow, *enough* already. Good night. These decisions are made almost thoughtlessly, automatically. They require little training and are primarily the result of habit-forming

And then there are more serious and possibly stressful decisions: change jobs, terminate an employee, race toward the yellow light, buy a car, sell a house, get married, or file for divorce. These decisions require thought and prove the value of a sound belief system, the basis for wise decisions.

Why do equally intelligent people have such divergent beliefs about so many concerns? Each may have developed different beliefs about age, race, creed, color, sex, responsibility, human rights, propriety, privacy, politics, courtesy and respect, good and bad, right and wrong. Differences may be slight or great. How does all this come about? Each of us is raised in a different environment. Each of us is taught differently. We perceive many objects and events differently, and at times misperceive.

One's belief system includes what is commonly called a conscience. It is stored within his unconscious mind. It is *his* set of beliefs, *his* truths. He was not born with a conscience, but he was born with the ability to develop one. However, the development in early childhood is involuntary.

The formation of belief systems and related feelings begins with early childhood events. In childhood one is taught by others whose opinions he respects and believes, right or wrong. However, as he matures, he draws some conclusions of his own regarding significant events in his life. Some are in conflict with earlier learning. All are stored as unconscious beliefs. They

17

became reinforced by subsequent similar experiences. They are accumulative. Combined, they make up his belief system. One's own truths will bias or slant his listening, reading, learning, reasoning, and decision-making, at times for good, at times not.

In happy and constructive situations, a child develops positive beliefs and emotions in conflict with negativity. At times he feels loved and confident. He enjoys learning and changing, and in adulthood still does. However, at times the child's conflicting negative desires, beliefs, and emotions rise to interfere with otherwise good feelings, and will do the same in adulthood.

Feelings associated with those beliefs control his decisions and behavior. They drive and inhibit him. Negative beliefs and feelings are a source of illness, but fortunately, positive ones are a source of wellness.

One's truths or beliefs, however biased, are recalled when sensing anything fat, slim, tall, short, white, colored, angry, happy, sad, depressed, religious, young, old, criminal, political, etc. Beliefs may be irrational. "Everyone should vote my party line. I'm too old to learn a new job. People of that color are stupid. This is the best automobile. I can't quit smoking. Women are too emotional to be good managers. Anyone having that religious belief is condemned. God is punishing me. Sex is dirty. All politicians are liars. Nobody understands me. Nobody loves me. I'll never get well." However, *one can strengthen rational positive beliefs*: "I can learn this if I try. What someone says *to* me or *about* me does not make me any more or less. I know I can whip this cancer."

Academic education does not ensure adoption of a belief. It only illuminates and informs. Unconscious negative beliefs may interfere with that light and learning. They affect and may even distort or deny what is being read, heard, or taught. They bias sensing, perceiving, and consequently conclusions. With continuing learning and work, negativity can be overcome by developing and strengthening positive beliefs.

Developing Beliefs and Desires

Unconscious beliefs change or develop as a result of keeping an open mind, and of accepting new conclusions and newly accepted information as being true. Conclusions are accepted as truth, first logically and consciously. Next, if they are significant or repetitive, they are stored in unconscious memory, often in conflict with, or somewhat deviant from preexisting beliefs. Visualization (seeing desired results in the mind) and repeated self-reminders result in forming or strengthening positive unconscious beliefs. Hearing repetitive statements from a respected source will *develop or modify* beliefs. Most mothers seemingly know this.

Repeated for emphasis -- a significant experience is an event, the memory of which is linked with memories of unfulfilled desires, physical feelings, emotions felt at the time, whatever is perceptually sensed by any of the five senses, and whatever is believed or concluded during the event.

Insignificant experiences are quickly forgotten. Memories of *significant* experiences are stored in long-term memory. Suppose one is driving his new car on a downhill curve in the road. He sees a large tree ahead. He sees the trunk, portions of its many branches, thousands of leaves, and numerous types of undergrowth. Given nothing else, the experience is of no real significance and will very soon be forgotten.

However, suppose it is winter. He is driving the same road, now icy and slippery. He comes to the same downhill curve. He is foolishly driving too fast and cannot make the turn. Because of the icy road, the brakes are useless. The steering mechanism is useless. The car continues moving straight and runs into the tree. The driver stores memories of the fear, the hill, the ice, the curve, the tree and its bare branches, striking the tree, and memories of the physical pain.

Memories of a degree of the emotions may later be recalled each time he drives on any icy road, or each time he catches himself driving too fast. Driving down any curvy hill at any time, he may feel discomfort. If the curvy hill is icy, and if he sees a tree ahead and the car momentarily side-slips, he may feel panic fear. He has sensed a greater number of reminders of the fearful experience. Emotions will be felt more deeply.

Retention of illogical beliefs may result from misperception. Seemingly insignificant incidents during childhood may be misperceived as very significant by the child. The significance and effect of present experiences are relative to what has already been experienced. Someone raised in a ghetto may merely scoff at what someone else views as traumatic.

A man whom I knew to be a very caring father asked me to try to help his son, a recent college grad, who was working in a temporary high tech job. Coincidentally, for weeks I had periodically observed him at work. Co-workers termed him anti-social. He made no attempt to make friends. When co-workers approached him, he responded in a very unemotional manner.

During hypnotherapy, the only negative experience that he could recall had occurred at Boy Scout camp. He was standing by his father who was the Scoutmaster. The other kids were roughhousing in the distance. He told his father that he wanted to be with them. His father bluntly and without explanation said, "No. You're not like those other kids." His son felt crushed. He believed the words, but not what his father had intended. The belief carried into early adulthood. It inhibited his ability to relate well in school, work, and social relationships.

In therapy he came to understand his father's caring admonition and forgave him. His personality changed almost immediately. He became outgoing and congenial. He later applied for and was employed in a job with a high-tech company. Years later, his father informed me that within the next several years after therapy, his son had been promoted five times before starting his own successful business.

A very young child cannot complete the business at hand. His desires are not met. All too often he is not satisfied with the outcome of transactions. He wants to be heard, to be understood. "No one listens to me. No one understands me. They make me go to bed too early. I hurt. I'm angry. I try to explain. They don't listen. I want to hit back. I want to play with my friends. I want to stay up later. I want to eat what *I* want to eat. I want to do things *my* way. I want to run away but I'm too little. I tried. I went all the way down to the corner, but I got scared and came home. I'm trapped. It's no use to try"

Every young child is completely dependent on parents or other adult caretakers for food, clothing, and shelter. Every young child is in fact trapped in his childhood environment. A child's unfulfilled desires, beliefs, and emotions are stored in the unconscious, waiting to be recalled later in high school, college, the workplace, in family life, and in old age.

A child is taught not to display anger, not to be angry, *as though he could avoid it*. He develops a belief that he must not display anger. However he also develops opposing beliefs. He may often *feel* angry. Adults display anger. Why not he? He believes he should be allowed to act angry, but he is controlled by others. He must attempt to act, not as *he* wants and not as *they* act, but as they *want* him to act, His desire is unfulfilled. Time passes. As an adult he sometimes *dares* to fulfill his desire. He dares to display his anger *unless* he believes the consequences to be too negative. He may even severely beat his spouse. Who's to know?

IMAGINE. A child nicknamed Scooter tries to reason with his parents but they tell him to stop talking back to them. He wants to stay overnight with his best friend, but his mom does not allow it. He tips his milk and gets scolded. He feels unloved. "Mom is not fair." He accidentally scratches his dad's car. He is punished and feels angry. "Dad is not fair." At the swimming pool, Scooter is afraid to dive off the high board. Dad laughs at him. Scooter believes he is a failure. They always tell him what to do and what not to do. He must follow too many rules without *gradual and timely training*. He fears the consequences of disobeying. His fear keeps him from doing what he wants to do. At times, he feels ridiculed, put down. He wants to get back at somebody, anybody.

He begins misbehaving, mistreating his friends. He tries to stop. He tries to change. He cannot. He feels helpless. He does not like those feelings, the unfairness. He feels inadequate, a failure. He cannot please Dad. Other kids begin to mistreat him. He feels angry. He wants to "hit back," to "show them." He does not dare. He stores the unfulfilled desires, the feelings of wanting to react negatively.

Now he is an adult. Those stored feelings are waiting to happen. They may do *just that* each time he is reminded of them by what he perceives in his surrounding environment at any given time. If someone tells him what to do, laughs at him, or calls him a negative name, he reacts negatively. He may impulsively *overreact,* even *violently*. Even though he is an adult and knows better, he misbehaves. He has the need to do so, the need to hit back, to be better than the other.

As one consciously recalls the memory of early experiences, he may be able to reassess what really happened. Merely becoming aware of childhood misperceptions may change or overcome an unconscious belief. As he reassesses, he develops new opinions, new ways of reasoning, new beliefs about what really happened. He concludes a new truth, but conscious and logical acceptance of a new truth may only modify or partially reduce a strongly held unconscious conflicting belief.

A married woman client, age 26, complained of sexual dysfunction. Merely thinking about sex elicited feelings of fear and anger. During hypnotherapy she was requested to recall her last sexual experience and to feel the associated negative feelings. She was then requested to let her mind drift and find those feelings another time and another place.

She associated her feelings with age one. She said: "I'm standing in my crib in the bedroom. I'm one year old. Mommy and Daddy are in bed. Daddy is lying on top of Mommy. He's hurting her. I don't know why he's hurting her. She's making sounds."

The client's unconscious had stored her misperceptions and the expectation and fear of being hurt if a man lay on top of her. She came to recognize just how invalid her perception had been. Her problem was resolved merely through the reassessment made possible by awareness and her adult reperception of the event. She later informed me that she had developed sexual desires and was no longer sexually inhibited.

Adults cannot determine what a child will or will not remember, nor the accuracy of his perceptions. Memories of experiences from birth and before may have lifelong effects, some positive, some negative.

It is not only childhood experiences that result in developing, storing, and reinforcing desires, beliefs and emotions. During adulthood, sudden violence, an accident, or any trauma may instantly overwhelm a positive feeling with one that is negative. One may believe he is safe in his home. He feels comfortable. An intruder breaks in and physically attacks him. He is seriously injured. This results in paranoid feelings with every sharp or unusual sound heard in his home, and perhaps elsewhere. Until now, he had felt safe, but his unconscious belief regarding the security of his home and street has suddenly changed. His unconscious now contains a belief that any surprising sharp sound signifies imminent danger, especially in his home. He may be startled by ordinary sounds. If he does not have further suddenly fearful experiences, the feelings will likely erode.

One may consciously want to embrace and sustain new and positive beliefs, but they will become automatic behavior only with repeated reminders. If one sees, hears, reads, or thinks them often enough, he may *unconsciously* accept them as *truth*. If he does accept them, emotions and behavior change. The old beliefs weaken and are overwhelmed by the new and stronger beliefs. Attempting too many changes at any given time will result in confusion and anxiety.

As an unfulfilled desire grows stronger, it becomes a psychological need. It may be a need to hit back, a need for love, a need to drive too fast, a need to help someone, or a need to give. It may be a need for recognition, to be wealthy, to call names, to argue and win, to exceed and be the best, or simply a need to feel better. At a given time, a desire can be compulsive, while at the same time impulsively feeling a conflicting desire to control that behavior. The desires are in conflict. One desire may be stronger at the moment because of perceiving more reminders, and having stronger good feelings *about* that desire. Tomorrow in a different environment, the opposite may be in control. Compulsive desires may compel one to become an artist, or to commit rape or incest, to buy or sell, to gamble, use street drugs, become a clown, minister, or champion, commit a violent crime, take one's own life, or run for political office.

After infancy, because of the complexity of interrelationships within the unconscious mind, it is unlikely that any specific feeling is ever recalled and felt by itself. A single reminder or precipitator may recall only a mild emotion. Sensing *many* reminders simultaneously in the current environment may trigger a deeply felt emotional rush, either positive or negative. One may be on an emotional high, or be severely depressed. Each is a composite of several feelings.

For many years the editorial page of Forbes Magazine, a noted financial publication, has carried an editorial page banner taken from Proverbs 4:7 "With all thy getting, get understanding." Understanding the associative recall of memories of unfulfilled desires, beliefs, and feelings will lead to an understanding of emotionally driven behavior, emotionally inhibited behavior, and emotionally caused physical illness. It will also lead to forgiving and to an understanding of the power of mind-over-body, and POWERFUL IT IS!

One person likes a specific color, another not. One person likes a classical music composition, another not. If, as a child, one often received loving care in a tan colored room, the color tan may later recall subtle feelings of being loved, of feeling happy. If a couple often enjoyed dancing and listening to a specific musical number, hearing it later may precipitate pleasant feelings. You may have observed one of a couple *smilingly* say, "That's our song."

Environments and Emotions

The environment changes as one meets new people, changes jobs, moves to new locations, or redecorates a home. All are different combinations, new sets of reminders of the past.

Walking down a long street, one perceives different aspects of the environment. As he changes from one environment to another he senses the differences, different reminders. As a result he experiences different sensations. As he walks, he sees different shapes, sizes, and colors. He smells different odors, senses different temperatures, and touches different objects. As a result he experiences different emotions, slight though they may be at times. Encountering different aspects of his environment serves to precipitate, to associatively recall different feelings, or to change levels of feelings already being felt. He may not realize why.

A feeling may suddenly become dominant. A change in what is being sensed may result in an instantaneous change in the emotions being felt. A nationally famous black minister, activist, and political figure is seen frequently on TV. He inspires black youths nationwide to accept the responsibility for working to improve their own lives. During an appearance, he said that one night while walking in Washington, D.C., he heard footsteps behind him. He said he was afraid until he turned around and saw a *white face*. The darkness, the sound of footsteps, the population makeup in D.C., and his awareness of the violent crime rate in the city had elicited his feelings of fear. Unconscious biases about both races had become manifest.

If one suffers with anxiety, stress, and breathing problems, he may find relief after moving to a new location, and not necessarily because of reduction of dust or pollens. He may have benefited by escaping from stressful traffic, a troublesome neighbor, disliked decor in his home or office, a noisy neighborhood, an unpleasant climate, an autocratic manager, or manipulative friends or family. In his previous location, the troublesome combination of precipitators had frequently triggered his stress. Many have now been left behind. It may take considerable time to encounter a new troublesome combination that could retrigger his health problem. In the meantime he is relieved. If he can maintain lowered stress, the symptoms may never return.

Any change in one's vocation or residence may recall anxiety and a fear of failure. The unconscious may have beliefs of: "Every time I try something new I get criticized. I can't learn it. I can't handle change." Yet another person enthusiastically looks forward to change and challenges, new places, new friends, new opportunities to learn, different homes and different workplaces. "It's a wonderful new life."

As surely as the world turns, it changes. Change is imminent. Change may be healthily viewed as opportunity for the better. If one is in the military or works for a fast growing company, he may make frequent and major changes of environment. Environmental changes occur through travel, through change in the workplace, different schools, social organizations, walking into the bathroom, or by merely turning one's eyes. *This book* is a part of each reader's currently and frequently changing environment. *So is this sentence* Missing punctuation or mispeled words may arowse a feeling in a reader, perhaps just a little contempt, subtle though it may be. Did you feel it?

As time passes, everyone experiences more and different events, desires, beliefs, physical feelings, and emotions. They are experienced around more people, more places, colors, sounds, shapes, tastes, and odors. One touches more objects with more parts of his body. Each type of emotion becomes linked to increasingly more sensory experiences.

Having *positive and pleasant* thoughts and experiences around many people, at many times and in many places, conditions one to feel good around many aspects of many environments. Current sensing of any of many different aspects of the environment recalls pleasant feelings. He feels good at work, at home, and in social situations. No matter where he might be, he has a very good chance that whatever he senses will recall good feelings. He feels good almost anywhere. Life is wonderful.

Conversely, another may have had an inordinate number of *unpleasant* experiences while sensing many combinations of things in a wide variety of environments. Too many times he may have been unhappy around too many people, places, and things. He has developed unpleasant feelings that are now associated with too many aspects of any environment that he typically encounters. He may have difficulty finding pleasant places to be. He may not feel good *anywhere*. This shouts, "Avoid running with losers." If feasible, get out of and stay away from unpleasant environments.

Repression of Painful Memories

Repression is an unconscious masking, a curb, restraint, distortion, or concealment of intolerable memories associated with extreme feelings of fear, guilt, shame, abandonment, anger, rage, sadness, being unloved, or any other unacceptable desires, thoughts, and emotions, or of events such as rape, beatings, or threats of death. The memories are blocked from conscious awareness because of a fear of refeeling them.

At the beginning of World War II, President Roosevelt said, "The only thing we have to fear is fear itself." One fears refeeling fear, but he also has a degree of fear of refeeling *any* unpleasant and emotionally painful feelings. A child fears refeeling the hurts. He develops an unconscious belief that refeeling them would hurt too much. Recall of any memories of the event would trigger the recall of feelings experienced during the event. Unconsciously, he does not ever want to feel them again. The unconscious represses memory of the painful experience and will not let him re-experience the full effect of the emotions. The unconscious has a stored belief that consciously remembering and feeling the full force of them would be too painful. He had wanted to escape from fear and emotional pain at the time they were repressed, and unconsciously still does.

A child's love for a parent may be strong enough to compel him to protect the memory or reputation of loved ones that mistreated him. Repression prevents the disclosure of abuse. Inhibition may result from beliefs of, "I love and respect him too much to tell anyone what he did. He would be so ashamed if others were to know." There is also a fear of losing his love. "I need his love. If I tell about the way he treated me, he won't love me."

While being sexually abused, a young girl's unconscious mind may store beliefs of: "If I do what Daddy tells me to, I'll be loved. I cannot tell anyone that Daddy did something bad to me or I won't be loved. If I tell anyone about what he did, Mommy will leave us. Daddy said so. I'll never tell." When the abuse stops, in order to stop feeling the emotional pain, she represses the memories completely out of conscious awareness.

A young woman experienced periods of hate toward her father and did not know why. In therapy her feelings associatively recalled memories of age six, and of stronger feelings while watching him cavorting in their swimming pool with a strange woman, both nude. Guilt followed the anger. "I'm not supposed to get mad at Daddy." She was able to understand, forgive, and love him without the interference of anger and guilt.

While repeatedly experiencing abuse, a child feels frustration, terror, and rage, and may feel unloved to a nearly intolerable degree. He is driven to inappropriate behavior. He does not want to feel the emotional pain. He wants to escape. He feels hopeless. He represses his identity and many of its memories. He may escape into a fantasized alternate personality, or worse. His unconscious still contains and feels the effect of his negative desires, beliefs, and emotions.

The new alter personality will soon feel miserable enough to want to escape into still another identity. Without successful intervention, multiple personalities may carry from childhood into adulthood. However, the symptoms may temporarily disappear and may not become manifest again until adulthood when a number of reminders are coincidentally sensed.

A more common form of repression serves another and essential purpose. It contributes to sanity. If one were unable to repress to a degree, many of his significant earlier experiences, recall of any feeling would automatically recall the memories of hundreds of experiences. His mind could not deal with the flood of information and emotions. He would also refeel physical pain. Imagine someone momentarily angry with another, and suddenly a lifetime of a series of memories of the feelings of physical and psychological pain come into awareness along with the anger.

To achieve physical, emotional, and spiritual health one must come to understand childhood beliefs and the resulting emotionally driven and inhibited behavior. He must come to unconsciously believe what it is that he logically and consciously understands. He then automatically forgives. He can forgive every offender that can be remembered.

With understanding and forgiving, one shall have no need to forgive those who commit moderately offensive acts toward him because he understands and does not feel offended. No one will ever be able to offend him with words. Stress will be reduced. He can expect to live longer and feel better while doing so.

Chapter 3
EFFECTS OF THE UNCONSCIOUS

Inhibitions and Motivations

What a child *feels* now will later to some degree be felt by him as an adult. What a child *believes* now will to a degree be *believed* by him as an adult. This is more than enough reason to learn about and understand children and how they develop emotions and beliefs. One can then understand emotionally driven and emotionally inhibited behavior, both of adults and children.

Unconscious desires, beliefs, and emotions may inhibit one from speaking his opinion, seeking help, attending church, speaking before a group, changing jobs, or meeting and making new friends. They may motivate him to become an artist, violent criminal, skilled technician, child abuser, liar, thief, corporate executive, or to seek the presidency of the United States.

Beliefs and emotions may limit him to menial jobs, welfare, or emotional dependency. They may inhibit him from seeking better jobs or working for promotion. They may motivate him to become a sport star, scientist, gambler, or drug addict. They may control his social behavior. He may be fearful, rude, possessive, autocratic, confident, kind, caring, or magnanimous. One's personality and habits result from, and are formed by, unconscious drives and inhibitions that are based on unconsciously stored desires and beliefs, and *how he feels about those beliefs*.

A child who receives moral teaching and training along with love, praise, healthy touching, and appropriate discipline, feels loved, confident, and secure. A child who receives abuse or repeated criticism and ridicule without ever being praised is robbed of dignity. He develops beliefs of being unloved, unworthy, no good, inadequate, and helpless. He lives in pain. Later as an adult he may demonstrate a wide range of negative behaviors.

It is important to come to believe that, *what is said to me, or about* me to *someone else, does not make me any more or less than I was before it was said*,[1] and further, what someone *thinks* about me does not make me any more or less. The next step is to forgive the offenders.

It is not one's fault that he has unconsciously stored negative memories, and that they drive and inhibit him. They started in childhood when everyone else was in control. If he has negative beliefs, it is not his fault. Nor is it the fault of his *offenders* that they believed, felt, and behaved the way *they* did. Understanding and believing this is essential to forgiveness and subsequently to physical, emotional, and spiritual health.

Mind and Body

On a TV talk show panel, a psychologist said that emotions never cause physical disease. None of the panel members challenged him. A clenched fist, involuntarily tightened stomach muscles, stomach pains, headaches, high blood pressure, rapid or arrested breathing, or tension in the shoulders, neck, throat, or chest are not the result of healthy and happy activity.

It is not unusual for someone to fear developing the type of disease that a parent had. Many of the handed down diseases may not be genetic at all. In an 1872 study, Charles Darwin wrote of the physical reaction of humans and specific animals while experiencing specific emotions.[2] He asked associates in various parts of the world to replicate his study. Some were on islands, some in jungles where no civilized person had previously been. Their studies confirmed his findings. They documented detailed observations of physical reactions to specific emotions such as anger, joy, and fear.

The studies concluded that persons of all races and cultures throughout the world, while experiencing specific emotions,

---

[1] How to be Your Own Good Samaritan. Otterholt, Howard. Ashley Books, Inc. Long Island.

[2] Darwin Charles. The Expression of Emotions in Man and Animals.
The University of Chicago Press.

reacted physically with astonishing likeness. They also concluded that specific body muscles react to specific emotions in a consistent pattern of responses.

What about the rest of the body? Do specific negative emotions affect each person's internal organs similarly? Why not? *Consider this.* Because of a parent's repeated demonstrations of his emotions that are related to his own physical problems, the children may develop the same emotions. Specific muscles are stressed. Since the children feel the same negative emotions as did the parent, based on Darwin's study it seems logical that the resulting physical responses would also be consistent with those of the parent. The word, specific, is repeatedly used herein to make a point. The study indicated that specific muscles tighten in reaction to specific emotions. It is not unusual for specific emotions demonstrated by a parent to be instilled in the children.

Suppose that in a child, as in the parent, those specific muscles pinch specific nerves and blood vessels. Pressure is also applied to specific neck and spinal bones that then cause further pinching of nerves. The specific pinched nerves lead to specific organs. The body's same specific organs and areas become dysfunctional. It seems logical that the child will develop the same physical illnesses as the parent had experienced. I.e., Emotions demonstrated by a parent are passed on to the children. As the children experience the same emotions as did the parent, the children acquire the same illnesses as the parent. "I inherited it."

Some illnesses seem to come out of nowhere. Clients referenced in the following abstracts and elsewhere in this book cured their own physical ailments coincidental with cure or reduction of the emotional problems.

A twelve-year-old farm boy had difficulty breathing. Over a period of several years he had been given several hundred serum shots in an attempt to relieve the symptoms of asthma. In hypnotherapy he associated his feelings while breathing, with the asthmatic feelings experienced at age six. He was in the box of a grain truck. Dusty grain began pouring into the truck. He began coughing and choking on the dust. He held his breath. He tried to climb out but failed. The grain was like loose slippery sand. He was terrified and felt trapped. His stepfather heard him scream, climbed up on the truck, and pulled him out. To my surprise, the stepfather sat beside me and regressed along with his son. He reexperienced the entire ordeal.

It was as though the child's unconscious had stored the beliefs, "I shall have breathing problems whenever I breathe dust, move my legs, or feel afraid, pressured, confused, helpless, or trapped." After reperceiving the truck experience, the asthmatic symptoms disappeared.

Another client, also age twelve, was experiencing fear regarding his health and suffered with severe asthma. He gasped for air after walking distances as short as twenty feet. He associated the difficulty in breathing with being very small and riding a bicycle down a steep hill. He said the brakes failed. In panic, he stopped breathing until he got the bike stopped. He next associated the feelings with a second nearly identical experience approximately two months after the first incident.

Awareness and reassessment of the early experiences resolved the fear and asthma. The therapy session was conducted on a Saturday. His mother's male friend later informed me that on the following Monday, even though the boy's leg muscles were weak, he amazingly had slowly run twice around a 440-yard track at school.

Several clients suffered from dizziness, especially while riding in cars. One of them would stagger after merely quickly turning her head to look over her shoulder. During hypnotherapy, each associated the feeling with dizziness just prior to birth. I explained to each that the experience was a fast prebirth ride to the hospital, including careening around corners.

In every case the dizziness symptoms disappeared after becoming aware of the causes. The father of one of the clients was the ambulance driver who had driven his wife to the hospital. She said she clearly remembered the *wild ride*.

Several clients in therapy for emotional problems had been told by their physicians that nothing could be done for their headaches, some chronic and excruciating. During hypnotherapy, each client associatively recalled the birth experience. Each had been squeezed around the head by forceps used by the OB to help the birth process. One client, while regressed back to the birth process, said a machine was pulling him. After reperceiving the experiences, the headaches disappeared. Mothers of several of the clients confirmed use of forceps by obstetricians.

Several women clients associated menstrual pains with well-intended maternal predictions that their daughters would experience pain because the mothers had, and because their grandmothers had. Others associated their pains with having listened to schoolteachers and older friends making similar statements, and others with reading advisory books. All had been predisposed to expect the pains.

After re-experiencing their "learning sessions," they no longer experienced menstrual pains.

A woman, age 55, called me early one Saturday morning and wanted to see me right away. She had been invited to a birthday party to be held that same evening. A few of her close friends were also invited. They had been coaxing her to attend. She said she wanted to go but could not face others at the party because of her appearance. She said she was feeling rejection, but also shame and guilt. She wanted to feel better about herself so she could attend the party. I told her I had other plans. She was pleading to be helped and persisted until I agreed to meet with her.

I was surprised at her appearance. Her left eye was rolled up and to the left. Her left cheek sagged as though paralyzed from a stroke. She had difficulty pronouncing certain words clearly, and her voice sounded strained. She had been widowed for two years. Her husband had been bedridden several years before his death.

During therapy, she associated the feelings of rejection, shame, and guilt with numbness in her face. She next associated the feelings with being in a dentist's chair several years earlier. She said she could not feel her cheek. The entire left side of her face was numb to the hairline and above. She was having a considerable amount of dental work done on the left side. The dentist had given her a second series of novocaine shots.

She next associated her feelings with being at home after leaving the dentist. Because of her husband's condition, they had been celibate for years. She said her sexual feelings were very strong. Though the left side of her face was still numb from the novocaine, she attempted to engage her husband in oral sex. He was embarrassed and very angry. He rejected all her attempts at apology. She felt guilty and ashamed.

Within the following year her husband died. She had become preoccupied with feelings of shame, guilt, and rejection. Her cheek and eye muscles became dysfunctional as if continuously numbed by novocaine.

During the brief period of regression and while she related the experiences, I watched her face transform to one of beauty. Her voice and speech improved significantly. She looked 15 years younger. When she was fully conscious, I suggested she go into a bathroom and look at her face. I heard her shriek, "I'm beautiful! I'm beautiful!" She ran out of the bathroom foyer and ran around the room in circles continuing to shout. She ran into a second bathroom as though she couldn't believe what she had seen in the first mirror. She repeated the display of elation, "I'm beautiful! I'm beautiful!"

Her symptoms had been made manifest by the unconscious memory of emotional and physical feelings she had experienced during and after the dental work. Linkages to guilt feelings and beliefs about the attempted sexual encounter were also in the unconscious. She was able to understand and rid herself of guilt.

At the party that evening, her close friends did not recognize her by either her appearance or speech. She had to tell and convince them of who she was.

She had been working as a door-to-door jewelry salesperson. During the following week, her sales tripled and continued to rise.

Six nurses were referred by a former Superintendent of Nurses, all from the same hospital. Each felt stressed and suffered with chronic shoulder and neck pains. During therapy, each associated the feelings of stress with negative emotions experienced in the hospital. In each case, one or more physicians had talked down to the nurse, had criticized, rebuked, and berated her. With awareness, understanding and forgiving, the pains were no longer felt.

A number of adults had problems with stuttering and stammering. Some associated the feelings with parents' or teachers' angry-sounding insistence that the child stop crying. Each child attempted to "choke off" the sounds.

Some associatively recalled having been ridiculed and repeatedly interrupted by parents or teachers while in the middle of words and sentences. One who stuttered related the problem to a fearful childhood experience in Alabama when he was caught drinking at a white man's fountain. Each began stuttering or stammering, but some not until early adulthood. Their earlier sounds of crying and attempts to explain and to be understood had been choked back. Later the sounds of attempted speech were choked back.

Reperceptions of early events led to new beliefs. Each came to realize that he did not have to hold back the speech sounds. Understanding and forgiveness led to resolution of the speech problems.

Minor Incident, Major Misperception

Even though raised in a reasonably healthy emotional environment, serious problems may develop. Parents are usually unaware of a child's negative perceptions. What appears to the parent to be unimportant may later have severely critical effects on a child.

A woman in her thirties was referred by her physician who stated that she suffered from extreme anxiety. She had attempted suicide. She was having problems both at work and in her marriage and was contemplating divorce. A number of years earlier she had been institutionalized for three years with emotional problems. At various times over the years she had been under the care of an even dozen psychiatrists and several psychologists.

She had recently been hospitalized for injuries received in an automobile crash. She had intentionally driven her car into the trunk of a large tree. During therapy I suggested she concentrate on the experience of driving the car during the time just before she turned toward the tree, and to find the feelings another time and another place.

Each of the triple asterisked paragraphs represents recall of a different earlier experience. It is the emotions being experienced in the present that associate with and recall the earlier experiences. Pauses of varying length occur between the recalls, from a few seconds to many weeks.

*** I'm feeling depressed. Hate my job. I want to get

away.

*** My mother died. I'm driving my car. I feel terrible. Going around a curve. I see a big tree in the lights. I'm going to hit it. I *want* to hit it........ I'm in the hospital....... Now I'm out.

*** It's my lunch hour. I met my mother in the park. We're sitting on a park bench talking. My mom has to leave.... She's walking away from me. I feel awful. I don't know why. I was so happy before she left. I love her so much.

*** I'm 5. Mom is sick. I love her so much. She turns away from me and she's walking out the door with Dad on the way to the hospital. (A minor incident.) I'm lonely. I want to be with her.

*** I came to visit Mom at the hospital. They let me in, but I can't see her right now. They're working on her. I have to wait in the hall. Sitting on a bench with Daddy. They're wheeling a cart out of the room next to Mom's. Looks like a person is on it. All covered up. I hear somebody say it's a woman who died…. I don't feel good.

Because the client had seen the body on the cart at the hospital, she concluded that people go to the hospital to die. (A major misperception.) Her unconscious mind associated the conclusion with the memory of watching her mother walking away to go to the hospital.

Seeing her mother walk away from her in the park associatively recalled the same childhood emotions she had felt when her mother had walked away to go to the hospital. She unconsciously believed that any time her mother walked away from her, she was walking away to die. She also had the unfulfilled desire to be with her mother whenever her mother left her. After her mother died, the client felt compelled to be with her. She felt compelled to kill herself in order to be with her mother.

After she had reperceived the childhood experiences, she reassessed what had happened. She forgave her parents for walking away from her to go to the hospital without explanation.

Although her marriage relationship improved significantly, she and her husband continued to experience problems. Her husband would not attend counseling sessions but she was happy, and able to tolerate his behavior. Her performance at work improved. She was soon promoted to a supervisory position. Shortly thereafter she was promoted a second time.

Inner Conflict

Why does one *ever* feel confused, indecisive, or anxious? One believes, but may also have doubts. One believes briefly but with certainty that a decision is right, but may very soon feel anxiety over it.

Inner conflicts lead to indecision, confusion, and unwise decisions. Two or more unconscious beliefs regarding an issue may be in conflict. The conflicting emotional beliefs and the feelings associated with each may go up and down like yo-yos. A person may have a long held belief from childhood, but may later be taught or conclude a conflicting belief. He has now developed inner conflicts. Unconscious beliefs of yes and no, maybe and maybe not. They reside in his unconscious mind. Inner conflicts may occur between early beliefs and those learned or concluded at later times.

A child develops beliefs from what he is taught or concludes. They may differ from what he was earlier taught or was conditioned to believe. As with adults, his thinking and reasoning are biased and at times distorted by old beliefs. He may reject what is true. He is conditioned by teaching and by repeated demonstrations of care, love, and understanding, but also by misperceptions, misinformation, threats, warnings, precautions, admonitions, neglect, abuse, or random negative circumstance. He has degrees of feelings associated with *each belief*.

At a given time he may believe he is loved. As expected, he feels good about knowing that. The next day he may believe he is unloved. And as also expected, he feels *unhappy* about knowing *that*. He may feel confident one day, helpless the next.

40

Because of his training he may develop good feelings about being able to overlook someone else's offensive behavior. He has good feelings about not hitting back. However, as a child he may also feel *good* about the thought of fulfilling his desires to get back, to hit someone, to *show him*. Those feelings may never be completely put to rest.

Behavior changes if beliefs are modified or overcome. Not all beliefs are in conflict with other beliefs. Although certainty is elusive, it is unlikely that any rational adult has a belief in conflict with $1+1=2$.

If a child is repeatedly exposed to conflicting views by those whom he trusts, he becomes confused and indecisive and lacks confidence. One parent tells him one thing, the other the opposite. The child has no reasonable options. He cannot win. He cannot please both parents. He is in a double bind. Double binds are crazy-making. He wants to and does *not* want to. He obeys while feeling disobedient. He begins to doubt. "I don't know what to believe. I can't please everyone. I can't please *anyone*. Why try?"

His mother may tell him that everyone should love and respect people of all races. She tells him to avoid street drugs. She tells him to show respect for others. She tells him it is wrong to argue. The child stores the beliefs, " It is dangerous to use street drugs. I'm never going to use them. I should love everyone. I should respect others. Mom is always right."

He is told to love and respect people of all races but he hears his father curse an entire race of people. He is told to show respect for others but he hears his mom call his dad a name and he hears them argue loudly and angrily. He is told never to use street drugs but he sees his father smoking pot. "What am I supposed to believe? I am beginning to believe that I should not listen to my parents." He has conflicting beliefs and desires. He does not feel good about any of them. "No matter what I do or say, I can't please both of my parents. My friends don't lie to me." And later a trusted friend says, "C'mon. Smoke it. Crack won't hurt you. It's fun." Anyone can continue the story.

He has a childlike belief that if he obeys one parent, he will lose the love of the other. A child wants the love of both parents.

He wants to believe and obey both, but how can he? Conflicting messages from parents or other authorities confuse a child, give him feelings of helplessness, of being trapped. He cannot comply with or believe both parents. Either parent can give conflicting parental messages through oral communications, by behavior, or by doing nothing.

As one approaches his teens, he rapidly improves his reasoning capabilities. Newly reasoned beliefs may be in conflict with old beliefs. As he encounters new and different sources of learning, he begins to believe more things in conflict with earlier learning, some of which were the result of childhood misperception. The conflicting beliefs are stored in the unconscious. They carry into adulthood. The unconscious has beliefs of, "I'm bad but I'm good. I feel guilty but it wasn't my fault. I know I can do that, but what if I fail? I love him, but I hate him for doing that to me. This is bad, but it feels good. Kids teased me and called me stupid. My parents criticized me. I must be stupid. But I know I'm not. I'm intelligent. I don't feel good around people because they are probably smarter than I, but I know they're not."

Later as an offended adult, he behaves in a manner about which he feels the best at the moment of being offended. His best feeling, or *least bad* feeling, may be associated with hitting back, perhaps physically, even violently, even *murderously*. Or he may feel the best about biding his time and getting revenge later.

At a given moment he may have several beliefs, each favoring a different specific behavior. Without awareness of the unconscious drive, he acts out the belief about which he feels the best at the instant of decision.

One side of an inner conflict may adversely inhibit one from taking common sense action. The other side may compel him to act or react favorably. He likely knows and believes which behaviors are appropriate, but he may also fear losing a friend by taking a moral stand. He may be too reluctant to refuse riding home with a drunk driver who happens to be his friend. He ends up injured in an accident, or worse. He may be too reluctant to terminate a stressful relationship. He might hurt the other's feelings. He stresses himself and becomes physically ill. He is too reluctant to leave a lawn party where street drugs are openly in use. "What would they think if I were to leave?" He is arrested along with the users. While still young, children must be taught and trained to take moral stands. Many will live longer.

When facing a decision, one has feelings about the desirability or undesirability of the consequences of his possible choices. Thinking about each of the possible choices may trigger recall of one or more beliefs, and either good or bad feelings. He picks the decision about which he feels the best, often without knowing or even wondering why he made that choice.

Today, one belief is stronger than a conflicting belief because of what one is now sensing and perceiving, or because of what he has very recently sensed and perceived. A moment later, or tomorrow, with a change of environment and different associations, he may suddenly recall some different thoughts and feelings that cause a different or even opposing belief to be the "right one," the one about which he at the moment feels better.

A parent needs to impart values, beliefs, philosophies, and ways of reasoning. Rationalizing must stop. Lines must be drawn. A parent's emotional need to be loved by his children or to be respected by neighbors, or by the sick side of society, may often be in conflict with common sense parenting. A mother may tell herself, "My daughter is running with the wrong crowd. I want to stop this, but if I do, she won't love me." A father may tell himself, "My son wants to stay out too late. His friends' parents let *them* do it. He is rarely home. He doesn't do his homework. If I ground him, he'll think I'm unfair."

Over a period of time, rethinking of responsibilities, probabilities, and consequences, and developing new philosophies, will reduce a parent's negative beliefs and inner conflict regarding the responsibility to teach and train a child to lead a disciplined life. A British psychiatrist, Karen Horney, believed inner conflict to be a primary cause of pathological emotions and behavior.

Intuition and Impressions

SCENARIO. A young girl's very loving father usually wears

43

brown clothing and often plays classical music in the home. Her feelings of being loved, happy, and secure become associated with hearing the sounds of classical music and with seeing the color brown. However, while still very young, she is often left with a physically abusive blue-eyed male babysitter who usually wears blue jeans. He threatens to kill her if she tells of the abuse. Seeing the color blue becomes associated with physical and emotional pain. Blue is bad. Brown is good.

Later as an adult she meets a young man to whom she is attracted. He is wearing a brown jacket and has brown eyes. He displays facial expressions similar to those of her father. She feels good near him and would like to continue the relationship. "Love at first sight." They agree to a dinner date. Wearing a brown suit and tie, he arrives in his car to pick her up. On the way to the restaurant they talk while listening to classical music. Having seen him and hearing the music, she feels great.

They arrive at the restaurant and are seated facing the band all dressed in bright blue. The stage is flooded with blue light. She recalls a small degree of the old negative feelings. While eating she occasionally glances at the band and its leader. While directing the band, several times the bandleader raises his arm in a manner similar to the motions of her early abuser. Without any remembrance of the abusive events, *stronger* feelings of discomfort rise without knowing why. She feels that she may have made a mistake agreeing to the date.

To avoid a confusing relationship, time is required to observe the other's actions, reactions, and inaction in many situations. Time is required to resolve conflicting feelings about another. As reasoning and new beliefs take over, old feelings gradually erode. If he is right for her, over time and after a variety of shared experiences, she may develop unconscious beliefs of: "He's a good guy. He's considerate. I like him. He treats everyone with respect. I like just holding hands and talking to him." Or if he is wrong for her, she may conclude, "I like him but he's conceited. He must always be right. He acts as though he listens, but he's only waiting for me to take a breath so he can interrupt. I'm going to avoid him, maybe." She may resolutely decide to end the relationship, or not. But the decision is based on a more realistic assessment.

Action, Reaction, and Overreaction

One may overreact to the behavior of others. Someone trips and falls against a person who reacts angrily and strikes the one who tripped. An observer is unable to hold back loud and long laughter. Both have reacted more strongly than is warranted in such a situation. Both have overreacted. One of them has displayed a need for revenge. The other has displayed a need to feel superior.

One senses elements or aspects of the current environment as they are encountered. Perhaps the most significant are interpersonal perceptions. They include words of praise, acceptance, criticism, ridicule and rejection, or the expression on a person's face. Also sensed are violent behaviors, the music of a concert violinist, a sermon, a comedy, a flavor, an odor, musical lyrics, or the hypnotic messages of rap.

The unconscious associates what is *now* being sensed, with what *had been* sensed, believed, and felt during earlier significant events. Through *associative recall*, degrees of previously stored desires, emotions, and physical feelings are brought into awareness. Recalling the memory of any part of an experience may recall any of its other associated memories. Suddenly one is what he was way back when. He may feel happy or sad, angry or forgiving, helpless or confident, and may react politely, rudely, angrily, or happily. A REMINDER. Recalled desires, beliefs, and emotions drive and inhibit behavior. This is so important in so many contexts, hence the repetition.

Resolving conflicting beliefs and feelings may require new ways of thinking about one, both, or several sides of a conflict. Some beliefs can be changed rapidly. In a University adult evening course on information systems management, I gave an assignment requiring brief research and a five-minute oral presentation of the findings. I asked if anyone would have a problem completing the assignment. Two students, a young man and a young woman each quickly said, "I can't do it." Each expressed fear of speaking in front of the class. During a break, I asked if they wanted to undergo hypnosis to resolve their problems. They did. I used part of a forty-five minute dinner-break with each.

The young man associated his fear of making a speech with his childhood perceptions of ridicule by an elementary school teacher, and by some of the students while he was in front of the class. Similarly, the young woman had repeatedly perceived ridicule at home while practicing reading poetry for a class recitation. Each had developed beliefs and expectations of being ridiculed while speaking to a group. They came to understand their offenders' emotional needs and forgave them. They completed the research assignment, made their speeches and enjoyed doing so. I had to interrupt the young man's speech. He had begun adlibbing and was so enthused he did not want to end it. Awareness of the truth followed by forgiveness had set them free.

At times one sees or hears incorrectly. At times he thinks and draws incorrect conclusions. At times he is so predisposed that he misperceives even the obvious. One may believe that he is sensing something that is not actually in the current environment.

IMAGINE. Early one afternoon on the other side of the city, John saw his red-haired neighbor driving his new white convertible. That evening he happened to mention this to his neighbor. His neighbor told him he had not left his office all day. John had been predisposed and as a result, "saw" his neighbor. The reverse is that he may fail to sense something that *is* in the environment. He overlooks a newly installed stop sign. He is predisposed not to see a sign in that location even though clearly displayed. He fails to stop. He gets a ticket, or worse.

Consequences, and the Control of Behavior

Why are some types of behavior *seemingly* controllable and some not? Since emotions drive and inhibit behavior, how can a person possibly control any of his behavior? In one situation negative behavior is inhibited by beliefs and by degrees of fear associated with a *quickly concluded probability* of negative consequences. In another situation, a desired positive behavior may be unthinkingly acted out because of a long-held unconscious belief of the *positive* consequences. "I believe it is right to behave morally. It makes me feel good." If one desires to do right, it is simply because of what is commonly known as the conscience. He has been taught and now believes that one behavior is morally right and good, or another is immoral and wrong. At times behavior is controlled by an unhealthy need for respect. "What will the neighbors think?" In a sense, this can be good. It helps promote moral behavior, *if* the neighbors have moral values.

One may jokingly, even lovingly, start talking to a friend. "Hey, shorty, ..." The friend does not sense humor. He is predisposed to sense ridicule. Immediately, conflicting beliefs are felt. However, he acts out the belief about which he *feels the best at the moment*. His childlike unfulfilled desire is to get back at anyone who ridicules him. However, he believes that he might lose a friend. His stronger desire is to keep a friendship. He feels better about the belief that he should treat his friend with respect. He angrily wants to interrupt him and call him a name, but *more so*, he does *not* want to. At the moment, he has a belief that he should not react negatively to a friend. That belief is stronger than the belief that he should get back at him. He tries to smile. He forces a smile. He *wants* to remain friends. He *fears losing a friend*. Because he has always hidden his feelings, his friend is unaware of the hurts.

Fear of believed consequences controlled his behavior *this* time, but *not always*. At times, he may encounter *many reminders simultaneously*, reminders of the old hurts. He angrily misbehaves even though he knows better and *wants* to act appropriately. He does what he *does not ordinarily want to do* because, at the moment, he has better feelings associated with *wanting* to do it. He may angrily criticize his friend. The *negative* side of his inner conflict is stronger at *that time* and in *that environment*.

Each adult faces situations similar to his childhood experiences. Because of that similarity, he associatively recalls memories of his childhood beliefs, feelings, and unfulfilled desires. In some situations, he is inhibited by a fear of refeeling

47

negative feelings. In others, he may be compulsively driven by emotional needs. He may react angrily, even to a beloved friend or family member. He may lose friends. He may even physically abuse his spouse. He has an unconscious belief of, "She won't do anything about it. I can get by with it." He may become a violent criminal, a pedophile, or a white-collar criminal, but *only if he believes he can get by with* it. He will have a weaker and gnawing conflicting belief that he might be caught. The stronger belief at any given time controls behavior.

One may consciously want to behave in a certain way, but because of his unconscious beliefs regarding consequences and morality, he may get a quick signal, "Don't do it!" He feels *better* about believing that he should avoid negative consequences than he does about *taking the risk of incurring them*. While at a party, he may want to join in the conversation but he has an unconscious belief of, "They'll laugh at me." He is inhibited by an unconscious fear of refeeling the criticism he felt during childhood. He wants to do something, but!

Suppose, while Jack is in elementary school, another boy calls him negative names. Jack feels put down, rejected, and angry. Other kids join in and tease him. They laugh at him. The name-calling continues. Each time, he reacts negatively. He feels hurt and helpless. He can't make the names go away. They hurt. He can't do anything to make the hurt go away. He feels inadequate. He wants to call them *worse* names. He wants to *get back* at them. His unconscious stores memories of the emotions, and memories of what he senses, and memories of his perceptions of the event. They are associatively linked in his unconscious.

Later as an adult, Jack hears someone call him a negative name. If he *understands* the name caller's emotions, the negative words have no effect on him. However, without understanding, Jack wants to figuratively strike out, but he has an unconscious conflicting belief coupled with fear. His behavior is instantly controlled by his unconscious belief of the consequences of acting it out, and the fear associated with that belief. He believes that the name caller would make him wish he had not been rude or violent. He fears the consequences of behaving *violently*, but he *may dare* to counter with *words*.

Awareness

Awareness is a state of being in the here and now, and of knowing what is happening. Nothing from the past is interfering. There is no fantasizing about the future. However the unconscious is never totally at rest. No one can ever remain in a state of 100 percent awareness. Lack of awareness is a major cause of relationship problems.

Unfortunately, awareness and concentration are mutually exclusive. One cannot be aware of what is happening around him if he is concentrating on a specific interest. This puts him in a double bind. During working hours, being aware of others and taking the time to show recognition may present problems. Awareness of issues *other* than the task at hand may cause errors. Yet *unawareness* of others' behavior in a company meeting can be a *debacle*. While concentrating on work, he may not be aware of how he is affecting others in the workplace but his unawareness is visible to others. *His unaware is showing.* He may not even be aware that he is or has been unaware. In a learning or work situation, concentration is often the higher priority.

In a work situation, one faces the reality that concentration reduces and even excludes awareness. However the work situation requires interpersonal encounters wherein it is essential to have a high degree of awareness. It is required to observe how others react. Only if he is aware, can he adjust his behavior to a reasonable degree to meet others' reasonable expectations. It follows that this precludes allowing one's self to *deeply* concentrate on *anything* while interacting with others.

It is clear that negative emotions interfere with awareness, but so may the positive. An overjoyed person may be unaware of others' behavior, desires, or emotions. In social or intimate situations, if one is preoccupied with his own behavior, he is unaware of its effect on others. He simply may not have developed enough satisfactory automatic behavior to let him feel free and be aware. He may be too much *into himself*.

Decision-Making

One is faced with decision-making many times a day. To stay in bed, or get up. To go to work, or stay home. To turn on the TV or read, or both. To dine at home, or go to a restaurant. Many decisions are instantaneous and impulsive. One sees someone reach out to shake his hand. He instantly reacts. Decisions are sometimes physically protective. One hits the brakes quickly or crashes. One moves his hand quickly or gets burned. Pain conditions one to react quickly. The belief of the need to react quickly is so strong that the reaction becomes involuntary.

If one has had good experiences, and has formed beliefs founded on good information, his intuition will treat him well. His conscience has stored moral data and beliefs. His unconscious beliefs are in agreement with his conscious and logical decisions. He makes sound, timely, and logical decisions. However, if one's unconscious is filled with negative and erroneous beliefs, or if he is lacking in related knowledge, his intuition will treat him badly. Earlier learning and emotional experiences have a significant effect on the speed, quality, and morality of decisions.

So-called buyer's remorse is common. "I can't wait to buy this new car." He signs the papers. He feels good. "I have a new car!!" He takes the car home. He walks into the house and sits down. This is where he wrote all the monthly checks to pay for his previous automobile. He recalls the memories and the associated feelings. He has doubts about his decision. "I don't feel good. I wish I hadn't bought it. I wonder if they'll take it back."

It is unlikely that anyone seriously claims to be *always* error free. Many may have said it before him, but 65 years ago I heard my father jokingly say, "I have only made one mistake in my life, and that was when I *thought* I had made a mistake but *hadn't*." Wrong decisions may be the result of invalid unconscious beliefs, emotions, irrational reasoning, carelessness and oversight, trusting a wrong person for advice, or not

50

understanding the problem or the objective in the first place.

In important matters one may reason long and hard to arrive at logical decisions. Sustained concentration may not be possible at times. While one is attempting to decide, he is sensing aspects of the current environment. During the reasoning process, he reads, speaks, listens, observes, analyzes, or just quickly decides. Depending on the number and complexity of the considerations, a reasoning process may take a year, an hour, or only seconds. All of his senses are at work. He senses. He feels. He thinks. He remembers. He may even have physical reactions.

While he is attempting to arrive at a decision, he has mixed feelings. He feels a composite emotion regarding each of his choices. He tries to think objectively. He tries to make a logical decision. He decides. If he feels the best about *that* decision, he acts on it. As soon as one faces the need to make a decision, one of his beliefs may instantly dominate. He decides. A short time later when sensing something different, other feelings and memories may be recalled. A different choice will feel better.

He may believe his decision to have been logical but may not feel good about it. It seemed logical but he *feels* it is wrong. In an attempt to feel better, his unconscious will prompt him to rationalize and deceive himself or do whatever it takes to feel the best he can. He makes a different decision. He chooses the alternative about which he feels the best at the moment. Yet he may not feel good about his decision. He may not have had any good choices. The best feeling achievable about that decision may be the least bad feeling.

Unconscious desires, beliefs, and feelings associated with those beliefs win out over reason and logic. Most people demonstrate a reasonably moral belief system, but sadly, the trend gives cause for concern.

Chapter 4
CONFUSIONS OF EARLY CHILDHOOD

The Beginning

From childhood, one tends to hold on to unfulfilled desires, beliefs, emotions, and perceptions along with the memories of later reinforcing experiences. If one can understand child development and the subsequent behavioral effect, he will understand himself and others better. If he can understand a child's needs and expectations, he will better understand his own. If one can understand how to relate to children, he can better relate to the figurative child in another adult and in himself.

Suppose an infant is loudly and emotionally rejected. He hears the words and stores memories of the sounds. An emotional mother may talk loudly to her infant baby, "I wish you'd never been born!" He hears the words, but they are meaningless at the time. The memory of the words is retained in his unconscious. As he grows older he learns the *meanings* of the words. *That* knowledge is *also* stored in the unconscious and is linked with earlier memories. He now has an unconscious belief that his mother does not want him, and that she regrets that he is her child. He unconsciously believes that he should never have been born. He is a nothing. He feels worthless. Later during misperceived unintentional incidents of being ignored or criticized, he feels unwanted, unloved, rejected, and no good, all without knowing why.

Later, in his teens and adulthood, he may misperceive some ordinary statements as words of rejection. It is as though the unconscious is saying, "AHAH! I was treated like that way back when. It must be true. He really *is* rejecting me." His emotions quickly rise. He feels frustrated, angry, unloved, rejected, depressed, and helpless. The result is as if the infant, even not yet born, had understood the words and the speaker's intent at the time the words were first heard. A parent cannot overdo the speaking of positive affirmations to a child from before birth until his teens.

Holding her infant daughter, a mother may say to a friend, "I never should have gotten pregnant. I wanted a boy." Although those words are not yet understood, the child now has the beginning of growing unconscious beliefs of, "I'm no good. My Mom doesn't want me. I should be a boy. If I were a boy she would love me. If I act like one, maybe she'll love me. I want to be a boy. I'll try." Mannerisms may change. The desire and behavior may continue for a lifetime. The adult may not remember *ever* feeling or behaving differently. "I was born this way."

Predisposition

If a child perceives himself as being disliked and unloved, later as an adult he will be *predisposed* to believe that others dislike and are rejecting him even though no rejection is intended. He will misperceive. With each such encounter, he recalls a degree of the emotional pain from childhood. The beliefs and feelings of rejection are recalled again and again. His behavior becomes more and more negative. Others will then, in *fact,* dislike and perhaps *actually* reject him.

A child may experience early life in a positive, loving, and supportive environment, or in a negative, uncaring, and critical one. Typically a child perceives some of each. Memories are stored in the unconscious. "You bought me the ice skates I wanted but you didn't take me skating. You say you love me but you tell me to be quiet when I'm telling you something important. You played ball with me but now you're too busy. I showed you the birdhouse you taught me to make but you weren't interested. We go swimming but you won't teach me. Mom says she loves me, but I heard her say she wanted a girl. You take me to ball games but you won't take my friend, Joey. You never listen to me. I must be no good. But you're always saying I'm a good boy."

The Need to be Loved

Every child needs to believe a parent's love is genuine. Typically the unborn child is warm, comfortable, relaxed, hearing various sounds from the outside, hearing his mother's digestive system, her breathing, her heart beat and the intermittent swishing sound of the flowing of her blood stream. Suddenly the feeling of comfort is taken from him by birth. He is placed in a "glass box" in the hospital nursery, often left alone and feeling abandoned.

Busy nurses walk away from him when he has a need to be held, to be caressed, and to feel someone's love. He has an immediate need for that closeness. He is not getting it. The desire is not being fulfilled. The unfulfilled desire is stored in the unconscious because it was not resolved. He feels neglected and alone. The unconscious stores a memory of nurses' walking away. He is unaware of other children's equal rights to *their* demands on the nurses' time. He is unaware that he was not intentionally rejected. The memories of the perceived experiences are stored in the unconscious. There is no reasoning or understanding at the time. While he is an infant in the nursery, memories of the nurses' walking away become associated with memories of feelings of being ignored, unloved, and rejected. The nurses walk away when he "needs" them.

If Ken receives loving care, attention, and respect after being brought home, the conflicting *positive* beliefs and emotions overwhelm the early *negativity*. However, suppose Ken is *not nurtured* after leaving the hospital, and his parents are "too busy" to spend enough time with him, the negative beliefs and emotions are *reinforced*. In adulthood, his good friend suddenly and without explanation may walk away from him, a common experience for an adult. His good friend has suddenly seen *another* of his good friends and takes only a few steps to greet him. Ken is left alone. Even if left only for a brief time, unconsciously stored feelings of rejection and of being ignored are recalled. "I'm not important enough. Without a word he walked away from me. He likes him better." Whenever someone walks away from me they are rejecting me." With each misperception, the beliefs are further reinforced. The feelings get stronger. He feels lonely, worthless, and helpless. If reinforcement continues, he may display a compulsive need for attention and recognition and a longing to be loved. For a lifetime he may try too hard to please too many in too many ways.

Conversely however, sustained loving treatment after being brought home from the hospital nursery minimizes the effects of the birth and nursery misperceptions. Feelings of loneliness and rejection are reduced. They are made almost ineffective by the conflicting stronger feelings of love and affection. A child cannot be spoiled with genuine love. Permissiveness is not love.

As soon as a child can pull himself up to a coffee table, reach an electrical outlet, or crawl up a stairway he needs teaching and training. However, he may perceive the best intended and most skillful and caring parental treatment as unfair. An act of love and care taken for his safety may be perceived by the child as undue restraint, as over-control. Explanations are warranted as soon as a child can understand.

A parent may walk away when a child is attempting to communicate. The child feels rejected. Adults are often in a hurry. Parents may walk away from a child leaving him with a caretaker who is a stranger to the child. The first time of being left with a sitter may be confusing, even traumatic to the child. He may feel rejected, even abandoned. He now has formed expectations of rejection. Thirty years later he may misperceive *anyone's* walking away as *rejection*.

The Child Perceives – and Misperceives

A father may laugh when his child mispronounces or misspells a word. The child begins to develop a belief that he is not intelligent. The child may make a mistake. His mother says, "How many times do I have to tell you? Why can't you learn?" The child's belief is reinforced. He begins also to believe that he is not good enough for his parents, cannot meet their expectations. His father may have intended laughing *with* him, not *at* him. His mother was trying to get him to learn, but her love was misdirected. His self-esteem is damaged, perhaps for a lifetime unless there is intervention to change his belief.

A prematurely born infant's feelings of loneliness are amplified by confinement in an incubator. Nurses care for him through gloved openings in the incubator. He is rarely held. He is lonely. He is alone while others are treated differently. He does not feel loving closeness. After a week or more he sees more clearly. Through the glass walls of his incubator, he watches the nurses pick up and hold other babies. He cannot yet form conclusions, but he stores memories of the experiences. Memories of being alone, of being unloved, and of being different are linked together and stored in the unconscious.

The confined infant wants to reach out, to touch and be touched, and to be held. The unconscious stores the memories of these desires, these needs. For a week or more, he does not experience his mother's love until taken home from the hospital. He has felt unloved for his whole lifetime up to then. Later he has unconscious feelings of loneliness, of being unloved. He does not know why. He will associate the loneliness and being left alone as unfair. He will be predisposed to perceive unfairness during normal treatment. If he has been left in an incubator for several weeks, he will later likely cling to others at every opportunity. The need continues. He will try too hard to be liked.

In the home, an infant often experiences hunger, the pleasure of being held, of being fed, a feeling of being cared for, and of having someone respond to his needs. He will feel love but will also form conflicting beliefs and feelings if dropped, if the bath water or formula is too hot or too cold, if he is shaken, scratched, stuck with pins, or held too tightly. He may be tossed in the air, swung by his arms, and bounced on someone's knee too hard, too soon, and too rapidly. His brain is jarred, perhaps injured. He may feel pains of intestinal gas, teething, earaches, sore throat, etc. He doesn't know why he hurts. He expects someone to stop the pain. He misperceives the intent of adults. This is the beginning of conflicting beliefs that others cannot be trusted and do not love him.

A newborn infant is moved from a place of relaxation, comfort, and security. He is brought home. When he cries, everyone jumps to serve him. Crying brings quick responses to his demands for feeding, changing of diapers, and being held. He begins to recognize and feel a sense of power and control over adults. He acts as if he is entitled, and for a while, he *is*. The memories of quick response to his demands are stored in the belief system. His expectations of repeat performances set in. He develops a godlike attitude, but as he develops further, he must learn to recognize and respect others' priorities.

Every small child must leave the godlike attitude behind and face reality. If not, his expectation is further reinforced. He will have learned that if he persists, he can win, he can manipulate others. His unreasonable expectations will later be recalled. He may become an arrogant and compulsively controlling adult. He may become a demanding, manipulative, and autocratic spouse, parent, manager, "friend," neighbor, or member of an organization. Weaning a child away from his perceived right to command others to pick him up and hold, feed, or change him *right now* requires parental patience along with tolerance of his crying, frustration, and anger.

Childhood Perception

Perception is a moment-to-moment judgment or conclusion regarding whatever is being sensed by any of the five senses. Misperception is a biased and incorrect interpretation of what is being sensed. Beliefs are based on perception which may be biased to the point of misperception. Right or wrong, one retains his belief of what he believes he has sensed, even if it was a misperception.

A child not only wants to be loved, he wants to *feel* loved. To a very young child, mere *words* of love are not enough. Talk alone is not convincing. Unless love is demonstrated, a child cannot perceive love, does not feel loved, does not *believe* he is loved. Physical security, food, shelter, and other material things are only a part of a child's needs. Love must be demonstrated at times acceptable to the child for him to *feel* loved. Holding, hugs, smiles, kissing on the forehead, cheeks or hands, loving pats, reading aloud, teaching, playing, giving time and attention, respect, listening, and acknowledging even some of an infant's unintelligible utterances - these are the kinds of demonstrations that let a child know and feel he is loved.

If he does not perceive and feel the love he will seek it, perhaps compulsively throughout his lifetime. He will seek love, at times in inappropriate manners and by the wrong people. He may become preoccupied with the need. He may accept an offer of a deviant relationship.

If love is not demonstrated often enough, a child may feel that he is not pleasing his parents or others that may be significant to him. He feels he is a failure. He is trapped with his feelings. He loses faith in himself. If parents inadvertently break promises, he loses faith in *them*. He wonders why they break promises. "They are supposed to love me." He begins to doubt God who also is supposed to love him. "Those who are supposed to love me don't really mean it. Maybe I'm not important to them." He develops feelings of helplessness and low self-esteem.

The helplessness may turn into hopelessness. He believes, "Nothing I do will help. Things can't get better. I'll never get better. I can't talk to them. They never listen." Later as an adult he may feel helpless. He may be pessimistic about getting well, feeling better, or succeeding in *anything*.

The question is asked, "How can children raised in the same home, in the same family, even identically appearing twins, grow up behaving so differently from each other?" First, from birth, each child's environment consists of a different combination of elements. Each child's very first experience affects his perception of every future experience. Each child has different experiences in the womb and during birth. Immediately after birth, each child is already unique because of different first sounds, temperatures, handling, and amount and type of attention received in the delivery room and nursery.

Next, each child is a part of every other child's total external environment. Fred is part of brother Joe's external environment. Fred looks in the mirror and sees his hair parted on the right side. Joe looks at Fred and sees it parted on the left. Fred sees his hand move away from himself. Joe sees it moving *toward* himself. *Joe* is part of *Fred's* external environment. They affect each other's desires, beliefs, emotions, and subsequent perceptions and behavior. A child's behavior has a different effect on his siblings than it does on himself. Also, he perceives parental treatment of his siblings differently from what his siblings do. No matter how hard parents may try, they cannot treat their children equally. Because of individual perceptions and unconscious beliefs, the differences may be great in the eyes of the children.

Further, even if parents could treat their children equally, each child would have different perceptions and different memories of the same parental treatment. Still further, learning and other developmental experiences are encountered and sensed in different sequences and in different environments. Each experience affects perception of every later experience. Each child has his own biases, his own beliefs, only some of which are *intentionally* taught by significant others.

Last, each child's environment is different. It includes dissimilar friends, associates, and teachers. They, along with parents, grandparents, neighbors, and babysitters react differently to each of the children. Since each child's perception of his environment is different, each child within a family is different, sometimes to an extreme.

Although parents are the major and most significant influence, it is not they alone who affect a child's desires, beliefs, and emotions. A child's belief system is shaped by his perceptions of everything and every*one* in the environment. Many beliefs are learned from teachers, siblings, and young friends. Others are concluded as a result of his observations and analysis during a variety of other experiences. Each sibling has different perceptions, and consequently different memories of the family, the neighborhood, schools, entertainment, morality, religion, discipline, and the world.

Growing Bigger

Every young child is under the control of one or more adults. Every infant needs love and security and wants to be free of pain, hunger, fear, discomfort, and inordinate control. He needs respect and a degree of freedom to make choices. He needs to retain his dignity. He needs to communicate. He tries to talk to his parents. For whatever reason, they may not take the time to listen. He tries to explain but without having someone willing to listen he cannot make himself understood.

Too often and from too many he may hear without explanation, "This is right. This is wrong. Do what I tell you. Don't ask why. Don't ask so many questions. This is good. This is bad. Be this way. Be that way. Do this. Don't do that. You might get hurt. You'll get sick. Don't try. Don't compete. You might not win. You're too young for this. You're too old for that." When he asks *why*, he may hear, "Just because." " Because I said so." " Because Mother knows best." "You'll understand when you get older." And he does not like it. He resents being controlled. He feels offended. He is frustrated. Unresolved continuing frustration turns to anger. He is angry with the offenders. He stores the anger and the desire to escape from control. He wants to do things *his* way once in a while. His unconscious stores the unfulfilled desire to control. He wants to be the manipulator. Later as an adult he may compulsively attempt to be the manipulator. He does not want to be told, advised, or influenced in *any way* to do or not to do *anything*.

A child raised in a healthy environment feels the demonstrated love. He receives respect, and *feels* it. He is taught and trained to follow moral rules. He is recognized and praised for improving his behavior and performance. He feels and will continue to feel confident, loved, and happy.

Every child has a need to understand and to be understood. He experiences being disciplined at times. *If* he is disciplined with careful and caring explanations, he feels *loved*. However, as he gets older, he believes he has the right to accept or reject guidance. Parents face the decision whether and when to let go. The basis for decision is properly based not only on his age, but also on when and how much he has matured physically, mentally, emotionally, and judgmentally. Appropriately, he is gradually allowed to make decisions of increasing importance based on his degree of maturity and wisdom. Too many parents abdicate from their responsibilities because they hear, "Other kids are allowed to do it." Premature surrendering of control to a child endangers his future, yet waiting *too* long will put him behind peers of his approximate age.

A very young child does not yet understand reasons for parental responsibilities. He has little understanding of danger and of the parents' need to protect him. He does not understand parents' emotionally driven behavior. He does not understand circumstance, and that he must accept the randomness of circumstance with its sometimes unfairness. His understanding may come later, and with it, beliefs and *feelings regarding what he believes and understands.*

Chapter 5
PARENTING AND THE FAMILY SYSTEM

Negative emotions are more quickly resolved if the sources are better understood. Since life and its problems and joys start in a real or substitute family system, where better to explore? Careful consideration of what happens in raising and in being a child may lead to an enlightenment of, "So *that's* why I feel that way." Another light may glow, "So *that's* why I've been doing that."

The System

Family life provides a type of support unobtainable by any other means. Loving support in a caring family is felt by every member, most importantly by the children. They will feel it throughout a lifetime. This is the antithesis of "the sins of the fathers." Unfortunately, a degree of negativity is also felt.

The family is a system in which every action by each member affects every other member, either directly or indirectly. Positive support of one member by another ultimately has a positive affect on all. Every interaction among family members affects future interactions. Every communication affects every future communication.

A family system requires management. It may be the husband that plays the dominant role, however a housewife with several children in her complex and well managed home is more of a manager than generally accredited. The situation is more complex and demanding for *married* working mothers, and even more so for *single* working mothers. The desirability of married mothers' playing a dual role is debatable but is often deemed an economic necessity, or is rationalized to be so because of material desires. There are also a myriad of emotional needs that are fulfilled by work outside the home.

If family members are experiencing relational and emotional problems, they can be expected to identify and blame a specific member as the cause of the problems. One of the children may misbehave at home and in school. Other family members then single him out as the cause. Or a family member who uses street drugs, or alcohol excessively, may be singled out as the cause. Recognize that the family is a system. Each member's behavior affects every other member's emotions and behavior. Blame for past incidents accomplishes zero. Family members may be in a state of denial regarding their own respective roles and contributions to the family dysfunctioning. They are blamers without realizing. If any family member has a problem, the system has a problem. If one family member needs therapy, it is likely that all do, "except *me*."

Most relational problems in a family can be satisfactorily resolved only through f*orgiveness* and through careful and caring *communications*. If the family cannot resolve its problems, a skilled marriage and family therapist may be a necessary part of the process. This can happen only if there is a *mutual* desire to resolve the problems.

Spousal Relations

Spouses can live together for many years without really knowing each other, and without ever having honestly disclosed and discussed feelings. If there are relational problems, one may believe that the other is at fault and will resist change. If they have not previously communicated their feelings to each other, they can expect difficulty doing so. Emotions may inhibit one or both from openly discussing problems in the marriage. One or both may believe that trying is futile.

Communicate about what is felt *now*. Now is the only time things happen. Talking about *current* desires, feelings, and behavior is more meaningful than digging up the past. Once started, it will gradually become easier. It means teaching the other about desires, likes and dislikes, and limits of tolerance. It means listening to each other. It means giving up some old ways. Once agreement is reached, each can patiently remind the other if agreements and understandings are being or have recently been transgressed. Stay out of the distant past.

Negative desires, beliefs, and feelings from childhood get in the way of feelings of love. Feelings from earlier times in the marriage also get in the way. Each will have different memories of the earlier emotional experiences. Blaming, even if tactful, will only destroy the healing. If a spouse is a blamer, overly-biased, overly-defensive, cannot or will not stay on a subject, continually makes assumptions, cannot or will not hear, and will not face facts and logic, *any* attempts at productive communications may be futile. Understanding, acceptance, and tolerance may be the best alternative.

An argument is an exercise in futility. There is never a winner. If parents argue, it is a lose-lose-lose situation – father, mother, *and* the child who is only an observer, all are losers. Hearing parents argue gives a child feelings of insecurity and fear. He views it as fighting, as a forerunner to divorce, as a forerunner to losing the presence and love of one of the parents. He does not understand what underlies the disagreements. He may have friends whose parents had fought and divorced. He may expect the same result with his own parents.

Parental Responsibility

Considerations in child raising seem endless. It has been said that love conquers all. Whether it does or not, it is assuredly a very important aspect of living. Parents who love and care will *take* care. Every child needs to feel loved. He can feel it only if it is demonstrated in a manner that he *perceives* to be loving. And it must occur at a time when he needs it or can accept it, and in a manner pleasant to him.

A 35-year-old male client had never kissed a woman. In therapy, feelings of revulsion over the thought of kissing a woman associatively recalled the memories of infancy and the slobbering kisses on his face and mouth by his mother and grandmother. That was *their* way of showing love to the child. He had not perceived it as love.

To care for a child is to demonstrate love and respect, to use caution, to precaution, to supervise, teach, train, and more. Parents do not automatically know how to parent. It is said the newborn does not come with a set of instructions. Fortunately there are classes in parenting skills, but unfortunately, time, cost, or location may present a problem. Books or a support group may be satisfactory alternatives.

To reduce or eliminate a young child's *need for peer approval*, he needs to be respected in the home. He can *feel* this only if he is *treated* with respect. He desires respect for himself and for his friends. If a parent wants him to avoid certain other children, he can be told in private. He can be taught to show respect for others, irrespective of their behavior. He wants to be heard when he speaks. *Listening* is in order. It takes time *now*, but it saves time and avoids grief *later*. He will be prepared for future encounters with society, friends, associates, and employers, each of whom has expectations. He can be taught to ignore the words of rejection from his peers who are attempting to shame him into trouble.

Teach and Train

The Reverend Jesse Jackson stated, "Teach the children while they are still young." And we should, and more. Teaching may result in *knowing*, however it *may* not result in *doing*. In Proverbs 22:6, Solomon wrote: "Train up a child in the way he should go: and when he is old he will not depart from it."

Notice that in his wisdom Solomon did not just say, "Teach." He said, "Train." Some meanings of the word, train: to guide the growth, to condition, to discipline, to prepare, to *ascertain* action to bring about a condition. Training takes time, but consider consequences of *not* doing so. Even *without* teaching and training by parents, the child *will learn* and *will* develop habits, perhaps not always *good*. Look at our streets, our schools - our prisons. Proper training of the child will not only prepare him for the future but will significantly reduce stress in the family system.

Preparing children to lead a happy life requires informed action by parents. It requires effort, often at times very inconvenient. But consider the consequences of not taking the time. After food, shelter, security, demonstrated love, and health care, *training by parents* is the next most important part of raising children.

Steve Allen, a brilliant former TV star, said we should add a fourth R to teaching our children. *Reasoning*. Although not brilliant, for years I have believed that second graders should begin to learn philosophy and reasoning. The first time a child wonders, he is on the road to reasoning. Without guidance, he may develop a defective reasoning process. He knows nothing of biases. Sound reasoning is based on facts, and he may be unaware that his very young friends are not a reliable source for facts.

Mere *exposure* to knowledge does not in itself motivate a child to learn. Learning requires the creation of an environment that will contribute to motivation and learning. It is the parents' responsibility to provide it at home, and the teachers' to provide it in the classroom. And in a knowledgeable, wise, and moral way, school boards have the responsibility to facilitate, limit, and allow. Learning also requires that the learner has a perceived benefit, even though it may be only recognition for having learned. The reason for him to learn may require a very careful and caring explanation. If schools cannot satisfactorily explain to a child *why* they are teaching him specific subjects, why *are* they? If he is not interested, there will be almost no retention. It is also important that he believe that learning *can* take place, and that he *can learn*. The learner needs recognition that learning *is* taking place and that it *has* taken place, *if* it has.

Studies show that in the training stages, intermittent rewards are more effective than rewards given after each and every successful effort. The trainee begins to perform for the sake of a feeling of accomplishment, not just for an immediate reward.

If children are taught to be biased against those who are different, what may be the consequences? Where will they draw the line on acceptable differences? Tall, short, fat, slim, black, brown, white, red, yellow, and six billion different personalities? Children need to learn to graciously accept differences in races, colors, religions, age, gender, shapes, and sizes, but to realize that degrees of biases exist in everyone.

Although many adults have never learned to do so, the young can be taught to stay away from troublemakers and their activities. If police come upon a crime scene, perhaps one of vandalism, stealing, or pot-smoking, it may be difficult for them to identify the innocent.

It is inappropriate to accuse a child of lying until one is certain. Not *almost* certain. CERTAIN! False accusations have a severe and lasting negative effect. They cause a child to become overly defensive and unable to accept constructive criticism. He may come to believe, "If I'm going to be falsely accused of lying, I may as well lie." If a friend, or later an employer catches him in *one lie*, when is he to be believed? A friendship can be destroyed. A career can be ruined. Although many liars survive in Federal government and its agencies (been there), they rarely survive in business (been there too). Avoiding unsupported accusations and teaching him the consequences of lying may help him keep his friends *now*, and friends *and* a job later.

Unfair criticism is destructive to child development. Criticizing the child in front of others is even worse. Physical punishment or severe criticism of a child in front of others, and especially his friends, will later be felt as low self-esteem, sometimes coupled with social anxiety. Rage may be felt at the time but may later be repressed. It hurts too much.

In relating to either a child or an adult, to some degree the child in each of us is relating to the child in the other. No one is ever completely free of the child. Children deserve more understanding and respect than the child in each adult is able to give without first having acquired a deep understanding of unconscious drives and inhibitions.

Socialization

An adult not wanting to live as a recluse needs to have been, or needs to become socialized. One cannot live as an island. Humans are interdependent. People rely on people. It is in the *midst* of people that a child develops from infancy into early childhood, subteens, teens, early adulthood, adulthood, and into old age. As he learns and matures, he takes on some new and unique attributes, characteristics, and ways of being, believing, and behaving. In most everyday transactions, society tolerates only a small degree of uniqueness and eccentricity, and in some situations, none.

In adjusting socially, it is critical for the child to learn the importance of developing a significant degree of conformity. He needs to be taught and trained to selectively accept and adapt to many of the moral standards and expectations of society and of those persons who are significant to him. Among these are parents, siblings, other relatives, playmates, schoolmates, teachers, religious figures, and friends. A child needs to learn to be selective in his choice of friends and organizations, and the whys.

A child needs to learn the importance of honesty, discipline, moral and spiritual values, and respect for others and their rights, opinions, and property. Timeliness is critical. There is an old expression, *pay me now or pay me later*. Unfortunately, it is the children who will later pay dearly if parents do not pay with their time now.

Ideally, developing *acceptable* automatic behavior starts early and progresses gradually. With continuing guidance and support, the child can comfortably learn with each new encounter.

If he is allowed to misbehave for a long time, incorrect behavioral habits and beliefs are formed. "Since I have gotten by with it, I can get by with it again, and again." He then begins to behave automatically in a manner unacceptable to significant others and to society.

Later, he will unhappily learn that his inappropriate automatic behavior may not be casually tolerated by others. It displeases those whom he wants to please. If he drifts too far from others' expectations, he may be socially rejected, terminated from employment, or divorced. He then realizes the need to change but may have difficulty doing so. Attempting to change this habitual behavior causes anxiety. While attempting to please but failing to do so, he becomes preoccupied with his failure and his behavior. Because of his increasing preoccupation with himself, his awareness of the reactions of others is decreasing.

He ultimately realizes and feels the rejection. His self-esteem declines further. He feels a need for approval. In attempting to receive approval, he then devotes even more attention to himself. He loses awareness of how others are reacting until it is too late. He tries harder and fails again and again. Frustration sets in. Anger, helplessness, and even hopelessness follow.

However, if he matures at a healthy rate, he begins behaving *automatically* with *acceptable behavior*. This is partly because of his own observations, assessments, and decisions, but mostly because of training and the essential help and guidance of others during his childhood. If he perceives most of his conduct as being acceptable to others, he does not develop a need to be preoccupied with himself and his behavior. He expects it to be acceptable because it nearly always has been. This frees his mind to be aware of what else happens around him. Because of awareness, he casually and accurately perceives how others are reacting to his behavior, at times somewhat unique. If someone does not approve of his behavior, and if he sees the disapproval, he may or may not choose to attempt to change.

Only through *early and persistent* guidance with parental monitoring will a child develop automatic appropriate behavior. It becomes habit, impulsive, unpremeditated, and requires no conscious thought. It is unconsciously and suddenly motivated. It develops largely as the result of parental action, or inaction.

Yet all the well-intended guidance from parents and others cannot completely prepare a child for the unpredictable. He will encounter new situations never before experienced by him, and perhaps not even by his parents. They could not foresee the different and sometimes unique experiences he would later encounter, or the need to prepare for them. Depending on his desires, beliefs, and feelings, he may enthusiastically view new experiences as interesting challenges. Or, because of childhood failures followed by lack of parental support, he may perceive anything new as another opportunity to fail.

Expectations

Many adults fear change. For most of the young, *lack* of change would be change. The rate of change in the world is rising as a geometric progression. A healthy child wants to change, to improve, to learn, to reach out, to test, to try. Appropriately, latitude is allowed to the extent the child is able to demonstrate progressively more skills, responsibility, and sound judgment.

During parental training, a child has limits as to how much learning and change he can assimilate in a given time. Attempting too much at a given time only confuses him. Habitual behavior must be allowed to evolve gradually. Support and recognition will help motivate him. Orders and demands will not. He can adapt but it must be gradual. Too rapid change will cause anxiety and confusion. Similarly, if a manager in the workplace requires an employee to make too many changes in a limited time, the employee's anxiety will *assure* mistakes and failure.

While changing a behavior, the child needs to rest on a plateau for a while until the new learning and desire to change result in automatic behavior, or at least until frequently demonstrated. He can then move on to the next desired change. As with adults, he must be given time to adjust. He wants praise for progress. He needs surveillance, teaching, training, reasoning, and guidance. Learning occurs through exposure, reinforcement, repetition, and demonstrated parental understanding. If he does not get a parent's time and guidance, whose? Whose beliefs *will* a child absorb?

Because of not learning good study habits, a child suffers from lack of a good education. He may later develop feelings of anger with parents for not having insisted on his forming appropriate learning habits, and for his not having learned.

A child needs to learn to keep appointments, to avoid procrastination, and to understand the difference between excuses and reasons, but to listen to both. Expect a child to test a parent's resolve. "Mom, I'll clean my room tomorrow. Dad, I'll do my homework tomorrow." Parental toleration of procrastination exposes a child to becoming an *adult* victim of circumstance.

IMAGINE. An employee is to complete a critically important job by a certain time. He knows the deadline. Barring circumstance, he may have a very good idea of the latest starting time from which he can finish on schedule. If he has not been trained, if he has not been held accountable during childhood, his belief from childhood is, "Later is OK." Barring circumstance, he may have allowed enough time to perform the assignment, however he defers too long, during which time something happens that is beyond his control. Something other than the assignment requires his time. Something else is suddenly more important. Or suddenly the resources to do the job are no longer available. He cannot finish on time. His waiting has made him a victim of circumstance. He may learn an unpleasant and costly lesson regarding the consequences of procrastination.

A child needs to know that a parent has confidence in him. He enjoys someone's laughing *with* him but not *at* him. He needs to hear an apology for thoughtless or emotional offenses. Emphasizing his good points motivates him to demonstrate them. Knowing that they have been recognized gives him a higher level of confidence and self-esteem. If he has high self-esteem, he will not be afraid to fail and try again. He will not have the need to blame others. He will not become a gossip or a name caller.

Discipline is often thought of as punishment, but it is also an orderly way of behaving. It is the result of training. Rewards and withholding of rewards are important in training a child to lead an orderly and disciplined life. Merely a kind word or a small sign of love may be enough reward, however not every proper behavior should be rewarded. Society sometimes rewards positive exceptional performance, however it will *not* reward mere appropriate behavior. Society rightfully *expects* appropriate behavior. Behavior patterns previously deemed improper are now rapidly becoming acceptable. Our nation is changing culturally. Moral values are changing rapidly, and sadly not for the better.

Discipline

Parents may be too permissive. Some are not even aware of when, where, or how their children behave. Schools are *not allowed* to do much in the way of disciplinary action with students. Principals may have to be overly political to keep their jobs. Teachers simply do not have the time or authority to do the parents' job, nor should they be expected to.

Every child needs to learn the importance of honesty and of honoring commitments. He needs to learn that if disciplinary action is being applied, it is so that he will learn to live a reasonably disciplined life. For his own good now and later, he needs to learn respect for others and their property, for society's unwritten rules, and for the laws of God and man. A program of rewards and withholding of rewards is effective in a positive way. Unfair or harsh physical punishment may result in long-term anger and resentment.

If a child is to lead a reasonably disciplined life, he needs to learn the meaning of *self*-discipline. Inappropriate behavior in a school classroom reduces quantity and quality of education for all students in that room. Too many parents have abdicated their responsibilities. Some have *never accepted* responsibility. They use the schools as child caretakers or part time foster parents. They expect, or at least hope, that somehow as if by magic and without effort by the parents, their children will mature morally, socially, and academically at a normal rate or faster. They expect their children to pay attention, follow rules, and earn high grades without parental guidance and disciplinary action. Worse, some parents behave as though they do not care.

Some States have gone overboard in legislating against disciplinary action. They have made *any* form of physical punishment of a child a crime. Very early, a child must be taught and *trained* not to grab a cup of hot liquid, not to climb dangerously high, not to hurt a little baby, not to stick anything in an electrical outlet, not to play with knives, matches, or lighters, not to place small or sharp foreign objects in his mouth, and more. It is not possible to keep every dangerous item out of the reach of an active young child. A child must be taught and trained. It is my belief that a few loving and caring swats on the hand or rear in the interest of a child's safety are an essential part of training and raising a child, and that the law should allow it.

A child wants and needs explanations of parental

expectations, values, and standards. He needs to learn the importance of listening and reading, and of respectfully considering the opinions of others. A five year old can understand if given small pieces of the picture at a time. Clear understanding of rules and expectations does not just happen. Parenting includes distinguishing between and among a child's mistakes, carelessness, acting on misinformation, misunderstanding, and purposeful violation of rules and expectations. Unfair accusations result in mistrust, anger, a need to be defensive in later relationships, and a need to blame others for one's own mistakes and failures.

A parent and a child each have expectations that cannot be met if they are not known. Telling and listening are important to each. Mistrust starts when a parent does not meet the child's reasonable expectations of care, love, respect, and responsiveness. Understanding comes only with careful and caring discussion. If he is to try, he must first believe that what is expected is reasonably achievable.

A child may often test parents' limits. He tries to get by with violating parental rules. He wonders, "Have they forgotten? Can I get by with it?" After following a rule for a time, and believing the parent is not paying attention to the old rule, he may break it. If a child fails to remember rules and follow them, or tests to see what he can get by with, he will likely do the same in the workplace, but not for long in each job. A manager in the workplace cannot and will not tolerate such behavior. Rules remain in effect until notification to the contrary.

Too much control, too many rules and admonitions suppress creativity. If a child is continually told how, what, when, where, and irrational whys, he loses the reason to reason. If all his friends are chosen for him, he may not perceive any reason to develop social skills. Why *should* he if he does not want to be with the acquaintances chosen for him?

From Frustration to Hopelessness

Imagine yourself as a child in a family environment and with zero authority. You perceive two opposing authoritative

74

messages. You cannot comply with both. You cannot win. You feel hopeless. You believe that if you do not please your parents, they will not love you. But you cannot please both. Each of them wants you to behave in different ways. You have given up trying to convince them of anything. You silently plead, "What am I supposed to do? Why don't you understand what you are doing to me?"

Or, to understand a child's frustration, perhaps an adult ought to stay away from favorite events, avoid watching favorite TV programs, stop reading in the middle of interesting and exciting books, spend money only on vital necessities, stay in a room for prolonged periods with nothing to do, and eat foods he does not like.

IMAGINE. You remain at your present size. You live in a world of people 12 feet tall. They control all the food you are served, the clothes you wear, and persons with whom you may associate. "Don't tip your glass." The furniture is gigantic. "Be quiet." They tell you what time to get up and go to bed, the movies you may attend, if any. "Put the candy back." They interrupt or walk away from your explanations. They do not bother to find out who misbehaved. "Sit still." They discipline you even if you are not guilty. "Get off the floor." When you are standing in an elevator, they back up against your face. You are always being told what you may or may not do. "Close that book right now." You are dependent on them for food, clothing, and shelter. There is no way out of your situation. You are trapped. Having such experiences would lead to a better understanding of children and the development of their fears, frustration, anger, and helplessness. "Brush your teeth and get to bed – now!" You may have wanted to read without interruption. Who cares? Who understands?

A child may be criticized for doing things incorrectly, not quickly enough, or for not starting soon enough. He may not receive recognition for a task very well done. It is *worse* when he is accused of doing something he has *not* done.

"Don't do as I *do*. Do as I *say*," is not a healthy message to give to a child. If a parent behaves differently from his teachings, he is giving conflicting messages to his child. The same problem occurs when two parents each give an opposing instruction or direction to the child. He believes he is damned if he *does* and damned if he *doesn't*. He is in a hopeless dilemma. He has no out. The best he can feel is helpless.

Children raised in a negative environment rarely have choices in significant matters. A teenager may want a say-so at home. If he is denied, he tries harder. He perceives unfairness. He feels mistreated. He acts up in school. He perceives disciplinary action as being unfair. Now he is certain that he is mistreated. He cannot change things. He feels trapped in the family, trapped in school. He *is* trapped. *Every* child is trapped in his environment. The feeling is greatly amplified if there is violence or incest in the home. Staying in his current home environment, he cannot escape from the feeling of being over-controlled.

In wanting to escape from his feelings, especially if he is abused, he may deny his very painful existence by developing multiple personalities. He may run away. He may turn to drugs, alcohol, or even suicide, the final escape. If a parent hears a child even hint at hopelessness or suicide, HELP NOW *is not too soon*! It *may* only be suicidal ideation, i.e., he *may* only be *wondering* about it, but how can one *know?* How can one know the depth or degree of compulsiveness of a child's emotional needs? Feelings of desperation result in unpredictable behavior.

External Influences

Although some rap artists are positive and have wonderfully positive messages, many young rap or recording artists display anger, hate, racism, and frustration. They believe they have a message to give. The message affects the young. The message is perceived as, "Be angry. I am. Display your anger. I do. Drag others into your misery. I do. You cannot resolve your problems. You cannot get better." Some encourage the use of street drugs and even the murder of police officers. And they make millions. Congress is much too complacent regarding many issues and the courts have stretched their definitions and interpretations of freedom of speech far beyond any reasonable limits and far different from the intent of the founding fathers.

Rather than allow children to listen to negativity, one can better teach children *why* these so-called artists have the problems they do. *Inform* them, "Negative rappers cannot help having their problems. Their problems are the result of negative childhood. Do not listen to their messages of hate, blaming, complaints, and misery. Only negativity can result from words or displays of racist anger or negative emotional outbursts accompanied by too loud supposed music."

Why do children carry weapons? You likely know. It is because of low self-esteem and a need to feel power, to feel superior, or because of feelings of anger and a need for revenge. This prompts others to carry weapons out of fear of those who already have them. And what has happened to holding parents responsible for their children's offenses? Children observe countless movie and TV murders and countless hours of violence even before starting school. They see, hear, and then conclude and believe that anger and frustration are properly resolved through violence. This misperception becomes a part of the child's belief system. It is in conflict with what has been taught them by otherwise proper parenting.

In playing computer games and watching TV, the internet, and movie violence involving every imaginable type of weapon, a child gets emotionally involved. He imagines *himself* in the role of power, over and over again. Hour after hour he is vicariously living a life of violence. His moral beliefs are under attack. His early childhood need to control others is reinforced. He is developing and reinforcing the belief that it is OK to use violence to *control* others, or worse.

Computer games, TV, or screen performances may portray a violent criminal as a hero. A child is allowed to watch and listen over and over again. The observing child learns and believes that violent behavior is OK, and that he can get by with it. If he associates with the wrong friends or with violent gangs, they praise him for violent behavior. He feels *less bad*. He mistakes this for feeling good. He is receiving the wrong training, developing the wrong beliefs, building up to a lifetime of pain.

Without parental guidance and *watchfulness*, a child is

susceptible to running with losers or even being a part of troubled and troublesome group or a gang with its gang violence. He may learn and believe the wrong things. If his conscience has not stored and reinforced beliefs to the contrary, he may come to believe that crime and violence are OK, that flag and cross burning are OK, that one race, color, or religion is another's enemy. He may become a danger to society, but do-gooder activists protect and defend him and his "right" to incite others.

Parental teaching may be overwhelmed by a child's sustained exposure to street mentality and beliefs. Parents' moral teachings are desirably expected to become a part of a child's unconscious beliefs. But teaching and training by parents cannot completely overcome the hour after hour hypnotic suggestions of immoral and violent internet, TV, movies, lyrics, and rap. The negative effect of these types of suggestions can be avoided or reduced by prohibiting or limiting the child's exposure to them. The child recognizes parental authority as authoritative only if made manifest by the parent. It can and must be made clear to a child.

"But all the other kids' parents let them do it." So now the parent has another problem. Is a child to be prevented from going to a friend's house where he can watch and listen without a parent's knowledge? What are the consequences of not reasonably controlling a child?

The degree of control that each child has over his own behavior depends largely on parenting. It depends on the amount of *sustained and repetitive guidance* given regarding consequences. If a child believes that *consequences will occur*, and that they depend on his choices and his behavior, he likely will act accordingly. Parents are the major role players in defining and developing a child's moral conscience, but immoral TV, movie, audio and videotape, and many computer Internet teachings are in serious conflict with morality. Moral values will dominate and prevail only after persistent parental teaching, training, and guidance, and then only if the child's exposure to the negative influences is significantly restricted.

Sibling Rivalry

A sibling needs to feel loved when a newborn is brought home. The newborn necessarily requires more adult attention. The older child perceives neglect. He believes that he is purposefully ignored. This results in degrees of negative feelings of envy, jealousy, rejection, confusion, unfairness, low self-esteem, being unloved, frustration, and anger.

Sibling rivalry is real and will result if unfair treatment is perceived. Fair or not, at times every child will perceive himself as being treated unfairly. A parent can only do his best. If a new baby is brought into the home, visitors tend to shower attention on the newborn. While this is going on, siblings need attention. They need to know that they, *too*, are *still important*. Mere gestures are not enough. From the first moment the newborn is brought into the home, involve the older children in the care of the precious addition to their family.

A man in his early fifties had a compulsive gambling problem. He had emptied his bank accounts and maxed out all his credit cards on riverboat casino slots. It started with occasional evening gambling and turned into casino-gambling on his way to work. He was depressed, and desperate to rid himself of the compulsion. One of his good friends paid the 2000-mile airfare, meals, and expenses to enable him to go through hypnotherapy.

I started with the suggestion: (And now imagine you are standing in front of the slots with a fistful of $100 bills. You are feeling something.)

I want to play.

(You know the odds are against you. If you continue playing, you know you will lose.)

Yes. But I want to play. I feel so good when I hit a jackpot. Sirens, whistles, flashing lights. People gather all around me. Pat me on the back. I get a lot of attention. I feel good.... I want to play.

(You are standing in front of two slot machines with your hands full of money. You have a need. Find that feeling another time, another place.......)

I'm in the living room. I'm four. I'm alone in my chair. Rocking – rocking – rocking. Nobody wants me. They just brought my new baby sister home. They're all in the other room. They leave me here all alone. They don't care about me. It's not fair. They are not paying any attention to me.

He regressed to the same feelings in school and at play. He misperceived being rejected by other children. As we progressed, his face and forehead smoothened. During a two-hour period his mannerisms changed. I watched him take on the appearance of a happy and confident person.

He had come to recognize and understand that he had been holding his beliefs and emotions for fifty years. He realized that his parents had been properly caring for the new baby and that they were not intentionally ignoring him or favoring his baby sister. After hitting the noisy jackpots, the bystanders had briefly given him the recognition he needed. Forgiveness, along with recognizing the truth of his earlier perceived neglect, prompted the change in him. After the session he was cheerful and laughed easily. We met his friend for dinner. He commented on the change in the client's demeanor and facial expression.

His intuition, his unconscious beliefs had told him not to gamble. He knew he would ultimately lose. But he felt better about the belief that he should try. He might win. He might get attention. About a year later I was informed that he had made one last attempt at winning and had not gambled since.

Every Child Needs Slack

A child learning to run will fall a number of times. He will pick himself up. Each time he falls, he learns. He repeats the cycle until he can run with confidence. Even with and after appropriate parental guidance, a child may make mistakes in learning and doing *anything* new. As age-appropriate learning occurs, he has a need to explore. He is appropriately allowed to try new experiences and to make the less serious mistakes that predictably will not cause significant loss, or endanger himself or others. He wants some slack. By being allowed to do or try, he improves by succeeding and by learning from his mistakes.

If learning-experiences are inhibited or deferred, the child will have to go through the failing and learning process at a later age. His peers will already have learned. They will have learned ways of thinking, and the skills usually necessary to avoid the mistakes. All too often they will ridicule the late learner. It hurts. To avoid this, he needs to be given an appropriate degree of latitude as soon as he demonstrates the ability to handle it responsibly.

It is better that his learning and adjustments begin during early childhood transactions. If they do not, he will be uncomfortable in his teens and in ordinary adult transactions. Because of knowing and feeling his own inadequacies, he will try too hard to please others in business meetings, social relations, or a job interview. If as a child he makes mistakes and learns from them, he will later be more comfortable and confident around others.

A parent may fear exposing a child to competition and the possibility of losing. A parent may precaution a child too many times. The same parent wants to spare him from feeling bad about failing and will influence him not to attempt anything unless success is almost certain. This may prevent his later participation in many important types of experiences.

If he believes that failing makes *him* a failure, he may begin to fear taking the ordinary risks in life. He should be allowed to try to exceed his known capabilities in moral efforts that do not endanger himself or others. If he fails, it is the failure, the act, that should be discussed, not the child. He can come to view the experience as a lesson learned. He can be taught how to avoid repeating errors. He needs slack in his rope as rapidly as he learns to handle situations responsibly, morally, and with reasonable safety.

A child can learn to make decisions early in life, starting

with those not having predictably serious consequences. He can be taught to think and decide in terms of consequences. As he demonstrates good judgment, he may be allowed to make more serious decisions. Mistakes will be made. Discussions will help him to determine how they can be avoided in the future. He may already know.

He can be taught the possible consequences of joining the wrong groups. He can be rewarded at times for *attempting* to meet, as well as for *meeting* reasonable expectations. It is never too early to teach him moral standards and the importance of meeting them because *he* wants to, not because someone *else* wants him to.

Precautions

A child may act out in *school* because of his negative treatment at *home*. He may act out at *home* because of treatment received in *school*. His parents, other students, and perhaps teachers react in negative ways to his behavior. Negative moods and behavior may be indicators of relational problems in school. This warrants discussion with a teacher. Most teachers are available for meetings. Most teachers are qualified and dedicated, but not all. A teacher's negative treatment of a child can cause a loss of confidence for a lifetime. Being criticized, ridiculed, or interrupted by his teacher when he is speaking, will cause him to develop low self-esteem and a loss of confidence. It may cause speech problems. He likely will have a fear of speaking to an audience or in a group. A parent has a responsibility to learn what kind of person is teaching the child.

A young child spends many waking hours each school day with the same teacher, perhaps more than with either parent. The exposure to a teacher's influence is too consequential to ignore. The child's self-esteem is at stake. His identification may be at stake. His ability to communicate with and relate to others is at stake. Subtly and indirectly, his life is at stake. Stress kills.

Manipulation – A need to Control

No one likes to be manipulated, but children learn about

manipulation early. Parents respond quickly to infant demands. The child continues to make demands. Later he learns how to be a manipulator from observing his parents in *their* attempts to manipulate each other. He also learns from watching other children manipulate *their* parents.

A young child has not yet learned to compete with the parent in the reasoning process. If a parent manipulates him through too rapidly presented logic, nothing good has been accomplished. What has been done is to frustrate him. He is in a no-win situation. "I'm helpless. It is not fair. They don't listen. They don't understand." He stores the memories and emotions. He wants to influence, to convince, to negotiate, to win. If he is never allowed to win or succeed, he stores the feelings of being a failure and of the unfulfilled desire to control, to manipulate.

A mother may be the manipulator of her child. If she continues manipulating him into his teens, after he becomes an adult she will likely continue to attempt to manipulate him but he, too, has become a manipulator. Even though he is an adult, she believes she is able to win because she has always been able to win. Through long experience, she has become expert in manipulating him. If he resists, she will redouble her efforts. She will attempt to instill feelings of guilt. She *must win*.

If he does not allow her to manipulate him, she will play the game of being unloved. "How could you do this to me? I'm your mother. I took care of you. You hardly ever call me. You don't take me shopping. You should be ashamed. You have so much. You have your children and friends. You're never alone. You don't know what it's like. You don't love me anymore." She may find many ways to make her points.

The inverse is that parents lose control if they allow themselves to be manipulated by a young child. He pleads to be allowed to do, wear, listen, watch, eat, drink, drive, spend, attend, buy, play, stay, go, or stay late. "All the other kids are allowed to." He unhealthily needs peer-approval. He has a need to conform. He needs to convince others. Parents who give in to this are allowing themselves to be manipulated indirectly by those other children. Are other parents and their children setting standards and values? Is that what any parent wants? Are acquaintances setting standards? Parents must make their own moral standards known and *understood*. *Sustained* monitoring by parents helps a child to build self esteem based on moral values. This in turn will deter his falling under the immoral influence of one or more of his peers.

A parent may wish to live vicariously through a child, may want him to pursue a specific career, may want him to study certain school subjects to prepare for a specific career. In attempting to control a child's future, a child may be driven away from a career in which he could excel. He has heard too many admonitions. He does not want his parents to continue controlling his life. Drawing lines and refusing to be manipulated does not signify lack of love for an overly manipulative adult child, sibling, or parent.

A young man, age 19, had left home and traveled 2000 miles to get away from his father, the senior partner in a noted law firm. He had flunked the LSAT (law school aptitude test), a prerequisite for entrance into law school. He had been confused while taking the exam. His father had angrily criticized him.

At the time the son came to me, he was working in a very menial temporary job assisting a government social worker. He wanted to leave the job but did not know what he wanted to do instead. He had become disenchanted with the behavior of the people he was trying to help. He also believed he was underpaid.

In hypnotherapy he associated taking the low paying job with feelings of guilt. He was unconsciously driven to compensate for his guilt. He was trying to make up for the anger he had toward his father.

He associated his feelings while taking the LSAT, with those he had with an early experience. "I'm sh__ing. I'm sitting on the pot on the kitchen floor. First time…. I feel *confused*…. Watching Mom."

The next association was with sitting on his father's lap. His father was telling him that when he grew up he was going to be the best attorney in the State. The client was too young to have *any* interest in an adult career. His father's talking about it too early only confused him. He heard it over and over again. He felt confused and did not like the feeling. It made him angry. He began to hate the words law, lawyer, and law school.

After reperceiving the childhood experiences, he said he had decided what to do. He had come to realize that his father had been acting out of love and concern. He forgave him for the method used. He said he was going back to be a law clerk in his father's office and prepare for the exam. He called his father that evening and told him that he was coming home as a result of our session. The next morning, his father walked into my office. He had flown 2000 miles to hear the whys.

He said it was too much to hope that his son was coming home. He had to know that it was really happening. With his son's permission, we discussed the findings. The father said he had learned his lesson. Two hours later he flew back home. My client made immediate plans to return home. Several months later he wrote that he had worked as a clerk doing research in his father's law firm. He took the LSAT on the earliest scheduled date, passed and enrolled in law school. Both sent thank-you letters and gracious invitations.

Unrequested career "guidance" given too early and too often is perceived by the child as manipulation, as just another attempt to control, another frustrating experience. It is outside a child's area of interest. It does nothing to motivate. It may have the reverse effect.

Self-Reminders Strengthen Beliefs

For their own mental and physical health now and later, children need to learn about and understand emotionally driven and emotionally inhibited behavior. A child's emotions may compel him to be a name caller, to try to put another child down. Another child will come to react in an appropriate manner if he has learned and been trained to *silently* remind himself when someone tries to put him down, "I understand your emotions. I recognize that you have a problem. What you say does not change me unless I want to change. No one can hurt me with words. I know who and what I am and what I stand for. It is you that have the problem."

Most very young children are much more intelligent than is generally believed. They *can* learn about behavior and emotions. It is *adults* who need the *patience* and *perseverance* to cause it to happen.

Repetition of self-reminders reaches and modifies the belief system. As healthy unconscious beliefs become stronger, forgiveness becomes automatic. A child does not then unconsciously store new negative experiences and the associated negative emotions. In fact, he builds even greater understanding each time.

Child Caretakers Cannot Just Sit

Baby sitters are expected to be caretakers. Approximately 50 percent of mothers are employed in the workplace. Their time is precious and must be prioritized, and allocated accordingly. However a living must be earned. The working mother's child is precious and must be cared for. If she works, she must arrange for and usually pay for childcare even though the cost is a severe burden.

A parent or parents have a need to know their child's caretakers. The wrong caretaker can abuse a child physically, sexually, emotionally, and spiritually. Verifiable references should be requested and checked. Rules and expectations are important.

On the other hand, it may be that one's own children are to be caretakers for children of *other* families whose morals and values are unknown. Their homes can be visited. Expectations can be discussed. A potential sitter's "Ohhhhh, Mom!" must not preclude precautionary investigation.

It is important that child caretakers clearly understand the parents' rules and expectations. Appendix E contains a sample memo including some suggested statements of rules, procedures, and requirements.

Chapter 6
VICTIMIZATION

Behind Closed Doors

The number of incidents of family violence is increasing. Outsiders may be unaware. Victims of abuse need understanding and help *now*. Every reader, perhaps without awareness of the abuse, probably knows someone who is a victim, most of whom are unwilling to disclose, but who need help.

Any physically able member of a family may become violent and abusive. The same may be true of any member of the *extended* family, even a "little old grandmother." Any member of the family may be a *victim* of abuse. There may be no awareness of it outside the family. A spouse abuser may present himself appropriately in society and the workplace. "What a wonderful man. What a wonderful husband! He wouldn't do that to her. He just couldn't." One *cannot know* what goes on *behind closed doors*.

Even some of the family members living behind those doors may be unaware of the abuse. A spouse may be successfully hiding the abuse. Except for muffled crying while alone in his room, a little child may be silently suffering physical, emotional, or sexual abuse behind one of those front doors.

An angry and abusive person vents his anger on a loved one because he believes he can get by with it. If he were to commit an act of violence against a stranger, he could face more reaction than he can handle. He would likely be subjected to like treatment or worse. He realizes he could find himself flat on his back on the sidewalk, or in prison. Any tendency toward violence against non-family persons may be inhibited by an unconscious belief and fear of the consequences. Fear is often the inhibitor of acts of violence toward anyone who would be expected to react in a like manner. Unfortunately, violent reaction can occur in an instant as the result of a well-intended comment that is misperceived by a violent person.

One may wonder why a woman married a man having the

most terrifying kind of behavior. It is a further wonder that even though abused, she continues to stay with that mate. Still further, it is appalling that after she divorces her abuser, she marries another.

One reason. During a first meeting, a potential spouse unconsciously recognizes a potential abuser's very subtle facial expressions, voice intonations, body attitude, and body movements. They are *too subtle* to be *consciously* recognized as the behavior of a violent person.

The expressions, actions, and reactions are the result of the abuser's unconscious emotions. "We make our own faces". It is the abuser's facial muscle reactions to his often felt emotions that mold the expression. Repeated emotional positioning of facial muscles creates patterns for future facial expressions.

An abuser's emotions ultimately make the face of an abuser, perhaps recognizable only to the unconscious mind of one who has been subjected to, or has observed violence in the home during childhood. The one who recognizes will almost certainly not be consciously aware that the unconscious recognition is even occurring.

An angry person's emotions become manifest even in non-violent episodes, at times very subtly, in voice intonations, facial expressions, body attitude, and movement. The abused or observing child stores memories of them. If traumatic enough, memory of only a *single* violent event, even though unremembered, may be significant enough for the unconscious to later recognize subtle indicators of an abusers propensity for violence.

SCENARIO: An abusive man's future spouse, but currently a child, is raised in a violent home. Her father physically abuses her. She observes her father's abusive treatment of her mother. Without awareness that she is doing so, she stores the memories of him before, during, and after abusive episodes, including the times when he switches to demonstrations of repentance and love, even if feigned. She fears her parents will divorce. She develops an unconscious fear of divorce. She imagines losing one of her parents. She imagines the loss of love of that parent.

She observes her father during his feelings of love,

happiness, and sadness, but also a wide range of emotions from only frustration and slight irritation to violent anger, at times rage. Memories of the scenes and of his voice intonations, facial expressions, body attitude, and body movements are stored in her unconscious.

Each abusive episode is followed by apologies, regrets, and demonstrations of love. She develops conflicting beliefs, "Everything is O.K. again. Daddy loves Mommy even though he hurts her. He hurts me too, but after, he says he loves me. He says he's sorry." Much of this may be similarly repeated later in her marriage or in an intimate relationship.

As a child, she experiences cycles of abuse, each ending with apologies, words and demonstrations of love, and promises that the abuse will never happen again. She feels loved after every session of abuse, and she observes that her *mother* receives loving treatment after each abusive outbreak.

Stored in her adult unconscious mind are the memories of her father's expressions and motions, and the belief that she will be loved by abusive and even violent persons. She has repressed her memory of the violence that she had experienced or observed during her childhood. She also has feelings of helplessness. The memories of the emotions are too painful to remember.

She meets a man who may not yet have behaved violently but who displays attributes subtly similar to her father's. They denote the man's concealed emotions that will later become manifest not only in abusive behavior, but also in regret and episodes of demonstrated love. Her *unconscious* contains memories of desires and beliefs, "I want you to love me. I need your love. I know you will love me even if you abuse me." She becomes the battered spouse.

NOTE: A child may be raised in a near-perfect environment. Even if merely observed, *only one observed abusive episode,* followed by loving treatment of the abused, may be *so significant* as to have an effect similar to that of being raised in the violent home described above. In adulthood there may be no conscious awareness, no conscious knowledge, that it had ever happened. *Any* frequent physical punishment, even mild and very brief spankings, immediately followed by demonstrations of love, *may* also have a similar effect.

Tolerance Forever?

A woman may stay in an abusive marriage for reasons such as financial considerations, fear of her husband's threats, helplessness, concern for the children, or a need to be loved. As a child she may have been over-controlled. She developed feelings of dependency. She may have minimal or no job skills. She may fear loneliness. She may feel unloved by others, but because of her unhealthy belief system, she feels loved by her husband. It is a misperception. He is incapable of feeling or demonstrating true love. It is only another of his needs.

After each abusive session, she vows to leave her husband but she stays. He abuses her again. To prevent her leaving, he may threaten her. Childhood feelings are recalled. She feels afraid, angry, trapped, and helpless, but she also unconsciously believes that love will follow the abuse. It does, but he abuses her again. He again demonstrates his unhealthy need for her. She misperceives it as love. Her unconscious attraction to the abuser is reinforced.

During childhood, her unconscious mind had stored the belief that an abuser will regret his emotions, demonstrate his love, and everything will be O.K. It seems to be for a time. Her unconscious stored the beliefs and fears that her parents might divorce and that she could lose the love and security of her home. During childhood, she knows that she cannot leave home, cannot earn a living. As an adult, she still has the same belief with one or more conflicting beliefs.

Childhood feelings are waiting to be recalled. In her abusive marriage, one unconscious conflicting belief is that everything will be OK. Although unremembered, because she had survived abuse as a child, she has an unconscious belief that she can survive abuse in a marriage. There is a degree of comfort in this. She stays in the marriage. She is consciously aware of the beliefs, "I know I should leave. He's not going to change. I have to stay for the sake of our children. I hate him. What would I do without him? I can't earn enough money. He said it would never happen again. I can't leave him. I'm afraid. I'm frightened every time I even think about divorce. I have a child to think about. Where can I go?" Temporary homes for battered women and their children are available. The county information center can refer her to those who will help.

As a battered spouse, she goes through the same cycle over and over. She knows that she is endangered. She knows the children are endangered. She knows she should leave. She *wants* to leave and does *not* want to. She believes she can survive divorce, but has a conflicting belief.

She is inhibited by her feelings. She cannot leave. She fears physical abuse and fears a loss of financial security. Each time, he tells her he is sorry and plays on her sympathy. They make up, make love, and he vows never to hit her again. An endless cycle.

A woman living with an abuser already knows she is living with a person who is aggressive, angry, demanding, possessive, irritable, domineering, jealous, explosive, unpredictable, and very dangerous. He will also exhibit conflicts between vanity and low self-esteem. He promises to change but does not. If she accepts the role of a battered spouse, will he ever change? He may blame *her* for his behavior. How does one change such a person? If the abuse is unreported, what is going to make him want to change? People change only if they *want* to change. If he perceives consequences that are too undesirable to tolerate, he *will* want to change.

If the marriage problems and abuse exceed a battered wife's level of tolerance, she will begin taking steps to stop the pain. Leaving with the children is one option. Divorce is a probability if she can overcome her fear. If she divorces, the emotional needs remain. Unless she takes steps to resolve them, she will likely recycle. She may again be attracted to a man having the subtle signs that tell her this man, too, will control and abuse her, and demonstrate love to her. She has no conscious awareness as to what attracts her. She may again entrap herself unless she defers marriage until after she has had a chance to observe him in many types of situations.

However, in the dating stage, he may control his violent behavior out of an overriding fear that she would simply walk away from him. If she seriously considers remarrying, it is advisable that she attempt to convince him of the benefits of joint counseling prior to marriage.

Physical and sexual are not the only types of abuse. Similar endless cycles of *emotional* entrapment may occur whether a spouse is an alcoholic, a drug or other substance abuser, an obsessive gambler, or plays the tortuous game of emotional abuse. A spouse's attempts to influence the other to seek help are met with excuses, ridicule, or unfulfilled promises. It is not always the man who is the abuser. It could be a wife, a teenager, a live-in, or a nearby relative.

The Abomination of Child Abuse

A very young child may love and respect siblings, uncles, aunts, older cousins, grandparents, baby sitters, or frequent guests of baby sitters. Yet any of them may be guilty of emotional, physical, or sexual abuse. It may be that only the child and the abuser are aware of the abuse. After sessions of abuse, severe threats by the abuser instill such a feeling of terror in a child that prolonged secrecy is assured.

A male client in his early forties, had both emotional and physical effects as a result of sexual abuse by his female preschool teacher. She had molested him while he was on the toilet. After the sexual abuse, wielding a knife, the teacher had threatened to cut up the preschooler and flush him down the toilet if he told anyone. He was terrorized. He could not tell anyone. He felt trapped and helpless. The full feelings of terror and rage, and memory of the event were repressed for 40 years. Fear had caused the anger to be repressed even more deeply. The terror had to be resolved before his unconscious mind allowed the anger or rage to be felt. He believed that displays of anger would cause the teacher to think that if he was not afraid to display anger, he was not afraid to tell others of the abuse. He was afraid of the consequences.

A parent who physically abuses his child may have immediate regrets. He may attempt to compensate by showing love to the child. The person who gives the child pain, gives him a feeling of being loved, but also the unhealthy *need* to be loved. The child wants to *feel loved*. Without knowing why, the child may later become a masochist, or a slave in a deviant slave-master relationship.

A child's feelings of fear, sadness, guilt, and low self-esteem along with anger and even rage at God for allowing the abuse to happen will all be stored in the unconscious. They will be felt as a composite of feelings, an emotion. Rage may also be felt toward the other parent for not stopping the abuse. "She is supposed to protect me. She's my mother. If she *doesn't* know, she *should*. She is *supposed* to know. She betrayed me."

One who sexually abuses a child fears discovery. An abuser outside the extended family will likely threaten the child's life to prevent disclosure by the child. The abused child typically stores memories such as:

> I don't dare tell. He threatened to kill me. I don't like to feel afraid. He hurts me. I want to tell, but I don't dare. Mommy shouldn't let this happen. God shouldn't let this happen. They *should* know what's happening to me.

A sexually abusive father may threaten the child with, "Mommy will go away if you tell." An abused child wants to stop the abuse but cannot, does not know how. He is too fearful to tell anyone. He gives up. He is trapped. He feels hopeless. The child stores memories of physical feelings, beliefs, and emotions such as:

> I feel unloved. He hurts me inside. I must be bad. I feel guilty. If I tell, Mommy will leave us. No one knows. I'm being punished. But after he does that to me Daddy tells me he loves me. It's so unfair. God is unfair.

The pain of the emotions is intense. Once the abuse stops, the memory of all of this may quickly be repressed completely out of consciousness. It is as though the unconscious knows, "If I don't let myself consciously remember this, I won't feel the full force of those horrible feelings." Later, *without knowing why*, varying levels of those feelings may be recalled, perhaps often but not as intense.

Do not expect the abuser to stop of his or her own volition regardless of promises to do so. Unfulfilled desire, beliefs, and emotions compulsively drive the abuser. Until his problems are resolved, or unless he and the child are separated, abuse will not stop. If a child abuser remains free, other children are at risk. He is a threat for many years. Stop the abuse. Blow the whistle. One cannot morally protect *any* child abuser or suspected abuser. *If a child is being abused, and if one does not report the abuse, more children will be abused. They will be emotionally scarred for life.* Is the one who fails to report the abuse equally guilty of the future abuse?

Look Beyond the Fantasy

A trial jury hears a child tell of abuse. He tells them of objects and events. They hear tales that clearly include fantasy. They often conclude that he has made it *all* up, that he has fantasized *all* of it. But *has* he?

A child who is abused is warned never to tell. He is threatened, perhaps with death, perhaps only with a scary warning that a parent will leave the family. The abuse and threats are repeated. The child is terrorized. He wants to escape. He wants to hit back. He wants to tell. He does not dare. Every time he thinks of telling, he feels the terror. He feels trapped and helpless, even hopeless.

As time passes, he has those negative feelings and memories around more and more things that he sees, hears, smells, touches, and tastes. In his unconscious mind, all of these things in his environment become associated with the fear, anger, feelings of rejection and betrayal, and helplessness. Soon those feelings are precipitated by nearly everything he encounters. Reminders are everywhere. He cannot feel safe and secure anywhere. Is it any wonder that his behavior changes? He is obsessed with getting away or stopping the abuse, but cannot. He wants to tell, but he believes he must keep it secret or he will be killed, or his mother may leave or be killed.

After being sexually abused, a young boy was threatened with a knife. He was told he would be killed if he were to tell of the abuse. Sexual abuse and knives are now associated in the unconscious. While dreaming or watching TV, he sees someone with a knife defending himself against a lion. It is very real to the child. The sight of the knife recalls the terror and abuse. The memory of the lion is now stored and associated with the memory of knives, his feelings of anger and fear, and of the sexual abuse.

Now he unconsciously associates sexual abuse, emotions, knives, fear, and lions. Sensing or consciously remembering any one of them may recall one or more of the others, each seeming real to him. *Some were*, but reality and fantasy are now associated. When he tells his story of abuse, he includes the lion as though the lion had been present during the abuse. Is such a fantasy believable? A knife? A lion? Can't happen?

This was an actual case. It had not gone to trial. The child had never told anyone. In therapy he remembered the offender had died while the client was still a child. Prior to therapy, he had no conscious memory of the abuse.

If such a case were to go to trial, would a jury believe *any* of the child's story? Not unless they were to understand the workings of the fearful child's mind. Defense attorneys may ridicule him. Juries may not believe him. Even the parents may express doubts. They must set aside what is known to be fantasy. Parents, counselors, attorneys, and juries *must listen very carefully to that which is not known to be fantasy.*

An abused child whose life has been threatened lives in fear even at the thought of the offender, and in terror at the sight of him. The child should not have to see the offender in a courtroom. To require it is not a fair or moral way to adjudicate. Further, an attorney's facial expression or body attitude or motion may be threatening to the child. Court procedures are in need of change.

Briefly and in part, examination, cross examination, re-exam and re-cross questions could be put on audio tape. A final live rebuttal session could be conducted under strict rules made clear by the judge. Questions could be asked with sight of the defendant shielded from the child. There are too many other considerations to include here, but a new and fair system can be developed and legislated. In child abuse cases, the accused should not have the right to face and frighten, perhaps terrorize his accuser.

Some parents unknowingly *set up* a child to be sexually abused. If a child does not receive demonstrated healthy love from parents, he will be vulnerable to receiving a combination of demonstrated love, gifts, favors, *and sexual abuse* from a relative, neighbor, teacher, religious figure, older sibling, or hired caretaker. Love to a child must be proven, not just spoken.

CHAPTER 7
UNDERSTAND, FORGIVE, and LOVE

First Things First

Understanding is the first step toward forgiveness. Forgiveness is real only when it is felt through believed understanding, not just expressed. If one is to leave the negative past behind he must understand himself and others, and unconsciously believe what it is that he understands. With unconsciously believed understanding, he can forgive most current offenses even as they are happening.

If he understands the emotional needs of others, he will significantly slow and even stop the accumulation of negative memories in the unconscious. He will view experiences differently, with understanding. He will not further reinforce unhealthy needs. Because of his believed understanding he will no longer feel offended by typical offensive behavior. He understands the emotional needs of the offender and the *whys*. As understanding grows, so does tolerance.

A REMINDER. One is driven and inhibited by unfulfilled desires, his unconscious beliefs, and the unconsciously stored emotions associated with those beliefs, i.e., how he *feels* about *each belief*. Beliefs began developing in childhood. They are associatively linked. Recall of one may recall one or more of the others.

Adults were in control when all of this started. It is not an offender's fault that he was subjected to infant and early childhood experiences. It is *not his fault* that he believes, feels, and behaves as he does, and that he cannot consciously control his behavior. (If you are a Christian and object to this, I remind you to again read Romans 7:!5-23.)

The biblical sins of the fathers are passed on to the third and fourth generations. How? A child's beliefs, unfulfilled desires, and emotions are largely determined by the behavior of the previous generation and how that behavior is *perceived* by the child. The effects are carried into adulthood. They become reinforced by subsequent similar experiences and *will determine* the adult's behavior. The same was true of the previous generation, and the one before that, and will be true of the next one, and the one after that. It is not the fault of the children that this happens.

Suppressed negative emotions punish mind and body. However, letting the emotions out, acting them out, does not dispose of them. Acting out anger is only a dress rehearsal for the next time. Anger cannot be managed. It must be resolved. It must be overcome with understanding. Only understanding and forgiveness can inhibit the symptoms of anger and put the emotional need to rest. If one can come to believe the above, he will have stopped slowly killing himself. He deserves to feel good and *can*!

An angry person may not want to forgive. He unrelentingly hangs on to the anger. He unconsciously desires vengeance. He has an unconscious need to hit back. Forgiveness is a surrendering of any opportunity for vengeance. "If I forgive I can never get revenge." Many feel and display anger when long-ago offenders die. "Why did he die? Why did he do this to me? Now I can *never* get back at him." However with believed understanding, there will no longer be a need to hit back.

The Bible emphasizes forgiveness many times. I have not yet found where it tells *how*. It also repeatedly tells of the importance of love. Loving others is impossible without understanding and forgiveness. Through unconsciously believed understanding, one can forgive, not only one person, or a few people, but *everyone*. If you are a Christian and do not want to forgive until the offender repents, read Matt 18:35 and Mark 11:25. Forgive *everyone - period*. No human can know whether or not another has truly repented.

Thomas Merton, a brilliant Trappist Monk, wrote:

> He who attempts to act and do things for others or for the world without deepening his own self understanding, freedom, integrity, and capacity to love will not have anything to give to others. He will communicate to them nothing but the contagion of his

own obsessions, his aggressiveness, his ego center ambitions, his delusions about ends and means, his doctrinaire prejudices and ideas. [1]

If one does not change, or does not work at greater self-understanding, it is because his beliefs and emotions inhibit him from doing so, or he does not recognize the need. "I have heard all that before. I have read all that before. I didn't do anything wrong. *They* did. There's nothing wrong with me. They just do not understand."

The problem started with birth and before, when others were in control. The negative emotions continue throughout a lifetime until appropriate intervention occurs. Too many times of feeling down may cause one to tell himself, "Enough! I'm going to do something about it." One can accomplish considerable mind renewal through relaxation, positive imagery, writing about his beliefs and emotions, and speaking and hearing positive affirmations.

Without believed understanding and forgiveness one may be carrying a load of unconscious feelings of anger, frustration, resentment, vindictiveness, a need to control, and a host of other negative feelings from childhood. They continue to accumulate. If one has *even a slight feeling of resentment* toward another, his health slowly deteriorates, often without awareness that it is happening. Forgiveness occurs only with understanding emotionally driven and emotionally driven behavior, and unconsciously believing what is understood. To avoid stress in otherwise stressful interpersonal transactions, he can repeatedly remind himself, "I understand." He can put small reminders on his bathroom mirror, his desk, the fridge, alongside his computer screen. He can remind himself of what it is he understands.

Merely speaking the words, "I forgive," is not enough to resolve negative feelings toward offenders. It is only a start. Without believed understanding of the offender's emotionally

---

[1] Merton, Thomas. Contemplations in a World of Actions. Bantam Books. New York. By permission of Merton Legacy Trust.

driven and emotionally inhibited behavior, professed forgiveness is meaningless. To feel forgiveness, the unconscious must contain memories of the belief that the offender could not help behaving in the offending manner, and that he *is worthy of forgiveness*.

A woman in her early 30s suffered from fear and was sexually dysfunctional. She experienced fear with features of paranoia merely at the thought of sex. During hypnotherapy, after several sessions of unconsciously resisting disclosure, she associated her fear with a time when she was home alone. An armed man wearing a ski mask entered her home. He physically assaulted, pistol whipped, and raped her. Memory of the experience had been deeply repressed.

After several sessions, when requested to do so, even in pretense she could not speak the words, "I forgive you." By steps she came to a level of believed understanding necessary for her to feel forgiveness. As the fear subsided, she dared to feel anger. She progressed to being able to speak the words but without meaning them. After many such attempts she was finally able to say meaningfully to her remembered and visualized masked attacker, "I understand and I forgive you."

At the point of feeling forgiveness, she just let go. Her arms and body visibly went limp from a relaxed feeling such as she could not remember ever having felt before. She later reported that her problems were resolved.

The forgiver *always* benefits. However, for the offender to get rid of guilt, he may have a need *to hear* that the person he offended forgives him. Yet, another offender may *not* feel the guilt and is *insulted* if forgiveness is offered. Telling such a person that he is forgiven only worsens the relationship. The offender may not have recognized his own offensive behavior, or has somehow convinced himself that he is blameless.

If *you* were offended by a loved one, he is worthy of your

102

understanding, your forgiveness, and your demonstrated love. You loved him once. Pure love is unconditional. You can love him again. Please try to believe that.

If the loved one that offended you is still alive and reachable, try to reach him. Merely *speaking* words of forgiveness is not enough. Hug him, but first ask if it is OK. If he is no longer available, *imagine* that you are *hugging* him even though you may not remember him. Forgive *everyone*. Does this disgust you? *If* it does, *you are your own proof* that earlier unconsciously stored memories of feelings rise to cause problems.

If at this moment you are resisting the suggestion to forgive, it may be because your unconscious mind is at work recalling old feelings of anger, vindictiveness, and of being told what to do. It is those kinds of feelings that stress you and interfere with everything you attempt. If you feel vengeful and want to hit back, you are carrying a load of anger. Barring violent behavior, it *directly* punishes only *you*. Your emotions have been inhibiting your understanding and forgiveness.

By now you logically and consciously understand, unless you have been inhibited from following the reasoning. If you were offended by loved ones, and if they are not available, or if they are deceased, imagine seeing them as you remember them. Imagine you are hugging them. Imagine you are telling them you understand. For *you*!

In a group counseling session at a prison, an inmate requested that I meet with him alone. I dismissed the rest of the group early. He had attended several group sessions and had finally expressed agreement and understanding that even though it *seems* that we consciously control our behavior, it is only because the unconscious agrees at the time.

He told of repeated beatings by his mother during his childhood. He said he hated her and expressed it vehemently. He felt rage. She had tried a number of times to visit him. He had refused to see her. He was soon to be released. I explained at length the development of emotionally driven behavior, which at times is abusive. He reluctantly admitted understanding. I suggested that he sit back, close his eyes and relax. I asked if he could remember an especially severe beating. He remembered one at age six. We proceeded as follows:

♦ Imagine that you are standing on a stool in front of your Mom. She has just beaten you. Imagine you are putting your arms around her.
♦ I can't *do* that! (He was very emphatic.)
♦ Please try. (I repeatedly requested this and reminded him that she had also been a child and had been driven by her childlike emotions. He finally agreed and said his arms were around her.)
♦ Imagine you are saying, "Mom, I understand and forgive you."
♦ No. I'll never forgive her. (He persisted, but so did I.)
♦ You told me that you understand.
♦ I do but I can't forgive. I'm in prison because of her.
♦ Try. (I decided to just wait.)
♦ I waited and watched. I saw the tiniest smile. It grew. Soon his face was radiant beyond my ability to describe. He slowly turned his face upward. Still radiant, he spoke, "Thank you, Jesus." A few tears rolled - his and mine. Slowly he opened his eyes and said, "I can't wait to see my Mom." I said, "And hug her." "Yes."

"Let me count the ways" that I have tried to convey or clarify what is in this paragraph. Forgiveness does not grant or imply approval of an offender's behavior. The offender's behavior is emotionally driven and emotionally inhibited. It is critical to understand that those emotions started during childhood when everyone else was in control. If the latter is true, and *it is*, who is at fault? Certainly not the offender. Look to the previous generation, and the one before that, and the one before that. Who benefits from believing this, from understanding and forgiving? *You* do. Some who have offended you, and at whom you may be angry, may have forgotten the offense, may even have forgotten that you ever existed.

Guilt

Guilt feelings are tenacious and pervasive. They are haunting. Attempted resolution of guilt through rationalizing, bending the truth, or of outright deceiving oneself will only make it worse. More inner conflict will be created. The unconscious has a memory of what actually happened.

Guilt may interfere with everything one does. It reduces awareness. Feelings of guilt are distracting. One stops paying enough attention to what he is doing. The effect of the gnawing and haunting interference is as though a little guy called *guilt* is sitting on one's shoulder saying, " Remember what you did? You don't deserve to take care of yourself. Don't pay any attention to your driving." "Drive through the red light. Get hit. Get a ticket." "Don't clean up the water and oil on the garage floor. Slip on it. Go ahead. It's OK to date him even if he *is* married. Do it."

It is as though one is being told, "This is not that important. Make your decision without thinking. You deserve the consequences. You are bad. You don't deserve any better."

If you are feeling guilt about anything, remind yourself that you were and are driven and inhibited by your unconscious desires, beliefs, and feelings. They started during childhood. Everyone else was in control. IT IS NOT YOUR FAULT THAT YOU *HAD* THE NEGATIVE UNCONSCIOUS DESIRES, BELIEFS, AND EMOTIONS THAT CONTROLLED YOU. FORGIVE YOURSELF. Remind yourself that they started when others were in control. You are worthy of forgiveness. So are they, but *forgiveness must never be used as a crutch, as an excuse to repeat inappropriate behavior.*

Tolerance

One need not tell those who misbehave that they are OK. They are *not* OK. It is not even OK that they are not OK. Their behavior is not OK. It is *not* OK that they affect others negatively. However, they cannot help being not OK. It *is OK* that they cannot help it. And one cannot change them. They change only if and when they recognize the problem and *want* to change.

One who misbehaves has unconscious needs. He may even have instantaneous compulsions. One can only accept that, and understand and forgive. Even though one forgives, he may choose not to tolerate.

One may increase his understanding of another person. IMAGINE that person is I. His tolerance of my behavior has increased. When he understands where and when I am coming from, he perceives my behavior differently. He recognizes I am coming from my childhood.

If I misbehave, if I offend someone, he is observing behavior of the child in me. My childhood desires have become adult emotional needs. If I attempt to criticize or put him down, he realizes it is I who have the problem. I cannot behave any differently from what I do *unless* I resolve the negativity or become aware of *fearful consequences.* My emotional needs are in control. I have not yet been able to resolve my negativity. As a child, I had the same problem. I am reacting to my own feelings of low self-esteem. He knows that what I say about him does not make him any more or less than what he was before I said it. It does not lift him. It does not put him down. He understands me. He forgives me. He may or may not choose to tolerate me.

He will not let me dump on him. He realizes that I do not like who and what I am. I want to feel better, to feel up, but I cannot - unless! The only way I can feel better is to feel superior by putting him down, by controlling his feelings. If I can put him down, I can feel above him, superior to him. Feeling only equal is not enough to meet my need. If I can control his feelings, I feel powerful. I have a need to. But if he understands my behavior, he knows it is my problem. He forgives me. He knows I am not well. His tolerance of my behavior is high because he understands my childlike problem, and because he remembers to remind himself that he understands. In understanding my problem, he will forgive me even as I attempt to put him down. He will no longer be reinforcing old negativity or accumulating new. He will not let me reach back into his unconscious and drag up old negativity that may interfere with his interpersonal relations. The level of his tolerance rises even higher.

106

If I see that I am failing at putting him down, I must try harder. I call him more names. I may use profanity. I act more contemptuous of him. But he understands that too. However he doesn't want to hear it forever. There is a limit to human tolerance. Even though most emotional problems can be resolved, there is a limit as to how long, how much, and how often one is willing to tolerate.

He may care for me a great deal, may even treasure our friendship, but my behavior has become too annoying. He has told me. He has warned me. But I persist. I exceed the limit of what he is willing to tolerate. I believe I am in control, at least temporarily. I need to feel the power. For his health's sake, he decides to take care of himself, number one. At some point, he wearies of my behavior. He may tell me how much he values our friendship but that I have gone too far. My behavior has neared his level of tolerance too often. He perhaps *could* tolerate my behavior, but why *should* he? No one has unlimited tolerance. Why should he allow me to stress him, to affect his health negatively?

He concludes that I am not changing. He knows it is not my fault that I resist changing, but he simply does not want to deal with it any longer. He has let me know that he has had enough of my behavior, but I persist. He requests that I stay away from him. If I refuse to withdraw, *he* may choose to do so. He bluntly tells me our friendship is over. He must do it. He must believe that he must take care of himself. Only then can he be the best and the most for those about whom he cares. He can forgive and care without tolerating my behavior. In taking care of himself, he will be better physically, emotionally, and spiritually.

If You Were Abused

If you were sexually, emotionally, or physically abused as a child and have negative feelings about yourself, about God, the abuser, or anyone else, please read this section carefully.

Abuse of children or the elderly is a crime. Your offender *knew* that he could be incarcerated, lose his family, lose his job and friends. He would be ostracized by society. *If* he could have consciously controlled his behavior, *would he have put everything at risk* for a few moments of deviant pleasure, or even briefer moments of uncontrollable anger? *Would* he? He *did*. Why? *He could not consciously control his behavior*!!

Believing the truth will set you free, but you may be resisting agreement. You feel better in believing that you should resist. Your biases may be influencing you not to try to understand, not to read, not to believe. You *can resolve* those negative beliefs and feelings. Understanding precedes believing. Believed understanding precedes the feeling of forgiveness. Forgiveness frees you from feelings of anger, resentment, rejection, and even abandonment. You can rid yourself of the emotional pain.

Anyone who has *recently* offended you in any way may have done it out of ignorance, or was driven and inhibited by unfulfilled desires, feelings, and beliefs that started during his childhood. The same was true of anyone in your *childhood*. It was true of anyone who abused you. His *unconsciously* stored desires, emotions and beliefs *were in control*. He was driven and inhibited by them. He could not help being the way he was and behaving the way he did. It is *not his fault* that those desires, feelings and beliefs were stored in his unconscious mind.

His behavior was not his fault. Why? *You already know*. It was because his feelings started during childhood while others were in control. It was not his fault that he has not gotten rid of or changed his negative feelings that drove and inhibited his behavior. He was inhibited by his unconscious beliefs and how he felt about those beliefs.

He has not been able to rid himself of all negative feelings. Who was to help him? If he did not seek help, why? It was because of not knowing where or how, or because his unconscious beliefs and feelings inhibited them from doing so. He is worthy of understanding and forgiveness. If you still have contact with him, even if only in writing or by phone, do not expect that same degree of understanding from *him*. *Be careful in expressing forgiveness to an offender* until you have determined that he *wants* to hear it.

You may have no conscious awareness, no recall of the

memory of earlier abuse. You may have only been *told* about the abuse you had suffered, that a parent or step-parent had abused you. Memories of the abusive episodes are repressed. You have unconscious feelings of anger, rejection, and unworthiness. You also have repressed unconscious feelings of *love for* him, and of wanting to be loved *by* him. You may never have had any adult awareness of it. Should this ever come into conscious awareness, please remember, his behavior was not his fault. He is worthy of your forgiveness.

You may be planning to *confront* someone who has abused you as a child. It is critical that you come to understand the other's emotionally driven behavior. In your mind, forgive the offender *prior* to the confrontation. Approach him carefully and caringly. Again, do not expect from him the degree of understanding that you now have.

Please be aware that the offender may not be able to handle the confrontation. And if you do not care that this might happen, you have not forgiven. You do not yet *unconsciously believe* what you logically now understand and believe. You have more work to do. The purpose of the confrontation is not to wreak vengeance, not to hurt the offender. It is to show understanding and forgiveness. It is *you* who will benefit.

Please, for the moment, do your best to set aside any anger, hurt, or contempt. Imagine you are looking directly into his face. Take the time to do it. Try to remember his appearance. Imagine you are telling him you understand. You *do*, or are you *denying* it? If you are, it is because of a stronger unconscious belief that you should resist. Only you can know the hurt you have felt for such a long time. It *was* not and *is* not fair, but the past cannot be changed. It *can* be *understood and accept*ed. Repeat this imagined encounter many times. As you continue, anger will reduce, understanding will grow. The pain will be put to rest. Forgiveness will change your entire life from the moment you *feel* forgiveness. You will remember without hurting.

If You Were Abandoned

If you were an abandoned child, I urge you to study the

remainder of this section. As you read, your biases may get in the way. However, if you are *searching* for *reasoned truth*, any resistance will erode away.

If you were abandoned or deserted by your parents, left to be placed in an orphanage, or if you were removed from your home and placed in one or more foster homes, you *unconsciously* feel abandoned, unloved, lonely, rejected, worthless, angry, and more. You hurt - *deeply*. Understanding your parents and forgiving them are essential to your health and happiness. Understand, they *could not handle the situation* they faced at the time they left you. They *could not handle* it whether out of anxiety, fear, greed, lack of ability to love, or whatever.

Their anxiety and fear became intolerable to them. They could not tolerate whatever they expected to happen. They feared accepting the continuing responsibility of parenthood. *You* may now be able to handle an identical situation, but *they could not*. Their emotions and beliefs compelled them to act as they did. *They could not handle parental responsibility at that time, and in that environment.* Their acts may be viewed as selfishness. One can only *be* a self with one's own needs, desires, emotions, and beliefs. It was not their fault that they had those beliefs and fears, those emotions, feelings of helplessness, and their compulsive needs and desires.

What we think or believe other persons should be able to do, will not enable them at all. It does not give them the capability. They could not consciously control their behavior. Would they have abandoned a beautiful young life if they could have controlled themselves? You are not being asked to approve of or condone immoral or inappropriate behavior, only to understand and forgive. It is for you, and for those about whom you care.

No one should *ever* have to go through what you have been through. But you can leave it behind. In your imagination, tell those who have offended you that you understand and forgive them. Speak the words even though at first you do not feel forgiveness. This may take many tries. The payback is wondrous. I have seen it so many times. If you are feeling resistance, fight it. Please. Tell them again. And again. It gets easier.

Although you may feel anger or discomfort with the thought of forgiving, you *can* resolve the negative emotions, but only by working toward, and by reaching believed understanding. Please try. Feelings of anger, abandonment, of being unloved, of resentment, vindictiveness, rejection, unfairness, or low self-esteem have no place in your life. You can put your negative emotions to rest through understanding the child in each of those who hurt you. It is so easy to say, "Don't talk to me about the child in them. They are adults." But when did the problems start, and why does *one* seek help and *not another?*

You are not sanctioning or validating their behavior. Their behavior may have been abominable, but as human beings, *they are not. Forgive them.* You will never regret it. If they are no longer on this earth, *visualize.* Again, imagine you are forgiving them, putting your arms around them. You can do it. Many others have.

Though they initially resist, I see prison inmates do this nearly every week. Many were abandoned, and worse. Many were shuffled in and out of up to a dozen foster homes and orhanages. Many were repeatedly beaten almost beyond belief, most often by step parents. They rid themselves of their hurts. You too can do the same. Emotionally and physically you will feel like a different person.

Search for Mother Love

Do parents or guardians love their children? Likely *yes*, to the extent they are *able* to love. Their love for a child may be completely overwhelmed by their negative feelings from the past. Do they demonstrate love? Maybe not enough in the eyes of a child, but if love had not been demonstrated to the parents, they likely do not know how to demonstrate it to a child.

One must come to know and believe that a parent demonstrates love to a child to the degree he is able. He may not know how. He may never have known love from others and cannot help being and behaving as he does, or did.

At times, the most loving parents' priorities are such that a child feels ignored and unloved. If love is not demonstrated often

111

enough to a child, his unconscious may store perceptions and memories of being loved every time he was held at the mother's breast during feeding, or while being bottle-fed. Because he is feeling safe, secure, and comfortable, an unconscious belief is being formed. His unconscious mind is beginning to believe, "You are loved when there is something in your mouth." Later, an unconscious, compulsive, and never ending quest for mother-love may later in life compel him to eat too often and too much, smoke, chew tobacco, constantly chew gum, or participate in oral sex.

Many clients rarely felt loved during childhood except at the table. They received attention while being taught how to use tableware. During and after meals they had briefly received much needed loving attention. They were smilingly told, "Good boy, you ate all your food. You drank all your milk." "You're a good girl. You cleaned off your plate." The statements may have been followed by hugs or loving pats. The unconscious desire to be loved and to receive approval strengthens the desire to eat. A compulsion to eat may carry into adulthood.

A young woman suffered with bulimia nervosa. While driving an hour to work each morning, almost unbelievably she would eat an entire carton of 24 candy bars. As soon as she arrived at work, she would go to the restroom, place a finger in her throat and purge. During therapy, she associated the compulsion to eat with a childhood experience of being praised for eating her green string-beans. She had to force herself to eat them. She perceived the attention and praise as a demonstration of love. She felt loved. When she was not eating she felt lonely and unloved. As an adult, she needed the praise and feeling of being loved, but *she could now choose* what she would eat to get her unconsciously needed "fix" of love.

Through adult reperception of the childhood need, her binge and purge problem was resolved. She was able to forgive her parents for their unintended offense.

112

To feel loved, a child needs demonstrated love. The child who *feels* loved can love others, now and later.

Love or In Love

In adult close relationships, what is deemed to be love may only be the result of mutual feelings of fulfillment of each other's emotional needs. Thomas Merton wrote on being in love:

> Often our need for others is not love at all but only the need to be sustained in our illusions, even as we sustain others in theirs.
> The expression, to 'fall in love' reflects a peculiar attitude toward love and toward life itself - a mixture of fear, awe, fascination, and confusion. It implies suspicion, doubt, and hesitation in the presence of something unavoidable - yet not fully reliable.... For love takes you out of yourself. You lose control. You 'fall.' You get hurt. It upsets the ordinary routine of life.... You become emotional, imaginative, vulnerable, foolish.... You are no longer content to eat and sleep, make money and have fun. You now have to let yourself be carried away with this force that is stronger than reason and more imperious even than business. [1]

What some may perceive as falling in love is only a fulfilling of each other's emotional needs. The display of those needs may range from subtle to brazen. The needs of one of the two who are "in love" fit the needs of the other. They complement each other. One may have a need to control. The other may have a feeling of dependency, a need to be controlled. One may be an optimist, outgoing, comedic with a broad sense of humor, and in need of a listener, in need of an audience. The other may be bashful, demure, serious, a listener, and in need of being lifted by others.

---

[1] Merton, Thomas. Contemplations in a World of Actions. Bantam Books. New York. By permission of Merton Legacy Trust.

As time in a marriage passes, those needs may become all too apparent, repetitious, tedious, and irritating. As evidenced by the divorce rate of more than 50%, what was thought to have been love is often later recognized as something very different.

Remind Yourself

Logical understanding followed by frequently repetitive self-reminders leads to unconsciously believed understanding. An offender is worthy of human forgiveness, but it is not to be used as an excuse to repeat an offense, or to offend anyone in other ways. One must work at remembering to think in terms of consequences of his own individual behavior. It is only through unconscious beliefs regarding morality and consequences that he is able to control otherwise negative behavior.

One can change by coming to terms with the past. It takes time and effort. What are the consequences of not taking the time and not exerting the effort?

In any moral and close personal, social, or business situation, avoid burning your bridges. Avoid slamming the door on the relationship. Keep your bridges up before and after you back away. You may want to reopen the door. You may want to cross back over the bridge. If someone else burns his bridge, you may want to help him rebuild it. Share the responsibility for the incident that separated you. If he repeats the behavior, you may choose to reconsider.

Can you consciously control negative emotions toward those who offend you? Only with unconsciously believed understanding. Most cannot. If you cannot, is it your fault? NO. Was it their fault that they offended you? NO. Are you worthy of understanding and forgiveness? YES. Are the offenders worthy of understanding and forgiveness? YES.

IF YOU CANNOT FORGIVE, CAN YOU LOVE?

If you have read this book from the beginning you *do* have

114

an understanding of human behavior. *Now*, if you have not already done so, please try to *forgive. Set yourself FREE. It is for you and for those about whom you care.*

Chapter 8
FEELING AND BEING BETTER

Accept Circumstance

In addition to understanding self and others, to feel one's best, one must come to accept the randomness of circumstance. The dictionary defines circumstance as a happening, an incident, a condition with external effects. At any time in life, circumstance may play a significant role. It could as meaningfully be called luck. Acceptance of circumstance leads to feeling better, the sooner after its occurrence, the better. One must learn to accept circumstance in this unfair world. Everyone experiences circumstance, some of it favorable, some not. It generally occurs randomly as to time and place.

With one person it may be, "I inherited so much money. I have a good job. I was offered it out of the blue. I'm so lucky. Why me?" With another it may be, "I'm always the unlucky one. The car I bought is a lemon. I get sick so often. My home was burglarized. I'm so unlucky. Why me?"

Circumstances are beyond control. They *will occur*. One does not choose his parents. He cannot control legislation by the various levels of government. He cannot control so-called acts of God. He cannot control the economy. All of these are circumstantial to him. Birth and early experiences were circumstantial him. If circumstance has treated him badly, it does little good to brood and ask, "Why me?"

Among the random variables regarding circumstance are time, location, duration, and consequences. Collectively, they are unpredictable. For health's sake, it is advisable to develop acceptable philosophies now before another negative circumstance occurs in one's life. Circumstance just happens. No one is singled out. Circumstance may favor some and not others. Circumstance and fairness have nothing in common.

Many argue that one creates his own circumstances, and in a sense he does. He has a degree of control in determining when and with whom he associates or comes in contact, and when and where he may choose to be geographically - a continent, country, state, city, street, building, or a room and wherein. He chooses or attempts to choose friends, mates, locations, vocations, avocations, automobiles, organizations, religions, homes, and what he eats. Circumstance relative to each of the above may happen at any time.

Things *will happen*. If choices work out well, he is happy. If they work out wrong, he can waste energy wishing things had been different. Or, he can accept circumstance and recognize his own role in exposure to it, if he had one, and learn from it. He can get on with living and *doing* and feeling better. Circumstance is circumstance is circumstance. It is not a rose, and he cannot change that.

Circumstance has a way of favoring those who wisely and not just intelligently select times and places that improve chances for favorable circumstance and reduce chances for unfavorable circumstance. Much of what happens can be traced to decisions to be in certain places, at certain times, with certain people, and to do or not do certain things. One also has a degree of control over being in a place where so-called acts of God and other circumstances are less likely to happen.

One has choices in determining the degree of exposure to many types of circumstance. He may choose either to live in, or to avoid locations that have had the most frequent earthquakes, floods, droughts, hurricanes, or tornadoes. He may drive or avoid driving on icy roads or in a snow storm or heavy rain. He may choose to go wading in a swamp in Florida's alligator alley, or not. He may choose to swim at a beach clearly posted RIPTIDE, or not. He may choose to fly a single engine plane, or not. He may choose to play a State lottery, or not. He may ride with a driver who is drunk or under the influence of drugs, or not. He has a choice. No one else makes him do anything. His unconscious is in control. It is how he *feels* about what he *believes* to be the consequences that determines his choice of decisions and behaviors.

Positive thinking regarding inordinate risk is in conflict with wisdom, with common sense. One may avoid street drugs, tobacco, or excessive use of alcohol. He logically knows the

118

possible consequences of their use but he may have a *conflicting* belief, "It won't happen to me." In potentially dangerous situations, thinking amiss that "I'm going to be OK" may be a denial of the reality of risk. "I can speed. My car is safe. I'm sober enough. Smoking won't hurt me. I can quit drinking any time I want."

One may attend or refuse to attend a party if he suspects drugs will be present. He may wisely choose to be in a location at those times when he is likely to encounter moral and caring people, healthy and safe conditions, and positive learning experiences. However, he cannot prevent invasion of those locations by others not of his choosing. An individual cannot prevent a drive by shooting. Individually he cannot keep murderous drunk drivers off the streets and highways, off his lawn, or from driving through the wall of his home. However circumstance tends to favor the wise and he can carefully consider, and use wisdom in reducing exposure to negative circumstance and in increasing exposure to positive circumstance.

At any time or place, *anyone* may become a victim of negative circumstance, or he may be lucky and be the beneficiary of *positive* circumstance. That is life. It could also be death. Acceptance of favorable circumstance is easy. One needs to work at accepting the random unfairness of negative circumstances, and doing the best he can with what he has.

Does he have better choices? Is there a better way? Is it better to waste time awfulizing? Or is it better that he overcomes the negative beliefs that inhibit the acceptance of circumstance, and that he accepts circumstances and the responsibility for the choices he makes that affect his exposure to any of the circumstances in his life?

Accentuate the Positive

In a classroom setting, a prolific author and one-time psychologist for the State of New York was asked about State residents' waiting two years for mental health treatment. He responded that as many were cured waiting in line as were cured through therapy. The first step toward cure was that each had recognized the problem. Had they not, they would not have sought help. This reinforces the belief that one can get better by recognizing and working through negative feelings. He can get better faster if he works at it persistently and frequently, and remains honest with himself in answering his own questions and doubts. Reasoning, positive thinking, healthy imagery, and listening to positive affirmations all lead to unconscious positive beliefs that allow one to feel his best.

Even though you have no identifiable significant emotional problems, write your answers to each of the following questions. "Who am I? What am I? Why am I? Who am I when I'm alone? Who am I without parents, siblings, a family? Who and what am I without a job or my business? What am I feeling right now? What do I believe are the causes? If I *had to give a reason*, what would it be?" Study your answers. Set them aside. Days later study them again. You may want to write more. You will learn more about yourself. It is not important enough? You don't have time?!? Remember Shakespeare's, *This above all, to thine own self be true.*

Imagery is a process of using the imagination to envision an object, event, or condition. Without imagery, there would be no houses, churches, roads, skyscrapers, automobiles, ships, or planes. Before a plan can be drawn, the object must be visualized in the mind. Before one would bother to draw a plan, he would have to believe it can be implemented or built. "I *see* it in my mind. I can do it. I can make it happen, I can succeed because I *see* it. I *believe* what I *see*."

Repetitive imagery of healthy activity and success makes them more believable. Imagery may have a very positive long-range effect. As the image is repeatedly imposed on the unconscious, the unconscious stores a memory of what is happening in the imagined healthful experience. What is being imagined can then be deemed by the unconscious as *believably achievable*. *Possibility* thinking is not enough. It fosters doubt. A better objective is to change thinking and belief from possibility to probability to certainty.

One can repeatedly imagine that he sees an action or

condition. Eventually, the imagery will contribute to believing. He will be unconsciously motivated by believing that he can succeed. "I saw it happen. I believe what I see. I believe I can succeed, I know I can." It becomes a believable message to the unconscious. Through repeated reminders, one strengthens his unconscious belief. Negative thoughts and emotions diminish. Self-esteem and confidence are elevated. "I *can* do it." "I *can* get well."

One can also reduce the effect of negative unconscious beliefs, and overpower them by bombarding oneself with logical beliefs and positive affirmations. Over many decades Norman Vincent Peale, a televised minister now deceased, emphasized the power of positive thinking. Repeated positive thinking can modify the unconscious. Positive thinking blocks negative thoughts. Persistence in positive thinking about an issue may lead to being not just a possibility thinker, but rather a certainty thinker. In addition to *thinking* positive thoughts, *writing* and speaking them will *reinforce* them.

One's positive beliefs are further reinforced by thinking positive affirmations while walking, driving, showering, lying in bed, or at any other reasonable time. Speaking aloud tends to accelerate the process of change. In addition to *thinking* the words, because they are being spoken, they are also being heard. Unconscious beliefs are rapidly reinforced. One may get some strange looks if he is talking while driving or strolling alone. So?

Positive affirmations while relaxed can build or strengthen positive beliefs. The undesirable belief of an inner conflict may be overwhelmed and pushed down to the realm of ineffectiveness. Repeated playing of an appropriate auditory tape can be very effective.

Organizations spend billions of promotional dollars on repetitive audio and visual affirmations. They use radio, TV, newspapers, handbills, magazines, internet pages and banners, T-shirts, toys, junk mail, email, fax, billboards, fence posts, utility poles, yard signs, bumper stickers, calendars, movie screen subliminals (now illegal), taxis, buses, musical trucks, benches, subways, trains, skywriting, package wrappers, store displays, blimps, skywriting, highway and street signs, free CDs, free audio and video tapes, golf bags, caps, and a myriad of free business gifts. Forgive the long list. It is presented here to help make the point that repetition *does* modify unconscious beliefs and desires. If it did not, companies would not be spending the billions of dollars that they do. *They know the process works.* They modify our desires and belief systems.

As our desires and beliefs modify, our behavior modifies. We believe and do as suggested by the ads. We donate, buy, watch, wear, listen, medicate, gamble, scramble, spend, send, broil, boil, eat, drink, breathe, drive, ride, jog, dance, lift, fly, click, search, read, print, mail, call, fax, e-mail, order, reorder, smoke, chew, use, abuse, sniff, spray, scrub, rub, brush, and even encourage others to do the same. They are now asking us to celebrate the beginning of the 21st century and the new millenium a year early, and are winning that one too. Even young children know that a century is 100 years in length, yet we succumb to the contagion of fascination with three zeros, or is it the #2?

They *know* the process *works*. We buy advertised products. Some are as advertised, some not. Some of us still smoke tobacco in the face of undeniable evidence that smoking slowly kills. We send money to articulate and persuasive TV evangelists, some moral, some not. We gamble money in state lotteries at unseemly odds.

Advertisers play on greed, pride, materialism, and other desires. It works. They have conditioned us to believe that we should respond. So why not be *greedy* about *feeling better*? Why not fulfill *that* desire? If the process has been proven, *why not use it to our own advantage*? Why not think, speak, listen, believe, and respond to affirmations that *we* choose? As referenced earlier, the Appendices contain suggested affirmations for your later consideration and use. Many have used them with significantly positive results. Thoughtfully add your own.

Positive Emotional Growth

While one is growing in understanding and believing, his behavior changes. He moves upward in a spiral as if sliding up a wavy wire in a vertical coil. The ascending spiral has continual

122

up and down waves, each wave higher than the preceding one. What is felt *now* is relative to what has been felt in the very recent past. While on a temporary down, one may not be realizing just how much positive change has occurred during the climb. If one feels down, he may be feeling better than he did on an old high. He can remind himself that *this low* is higher than the *previous highs*. The low will pass. A sign on the wall can serve as a constant reminder, *This too shall pass*. The stronger his belief, the more quickly it will pass. In his climb, he will occasionally pause to assimilate his changes up to that time, to let them become a part of his everyday life.

Life is not and will never be without problems. In one's eagerness to solve them, he may desire to work at solving too many of them at the same time. If he does not pause and take the time to assimilate what he has learned, or if he attacks too many problems simultaneously, he will start feeling shaky and confused. His thoughts will jump around from one to another. Instead, he can make a list and prioritize his tasks. He can work on resolving one or two problems having the highest priority.

Persistence and patience are important. After resolving a high priority problem, others may seem to worsen. Still others may have disappeared. Priorities may have changed. This is not the time to let oneself feel discouraged. It is time to reprioritize and *get to work* at renewing the mind. It is time now to resolve to continue working at feeling better. *With work*, it *will happen*.

Have patience. Remind yourself often of your understanding. And as you grow, avoid turning back. Avoid turning into a pillar of salt.

Limits

You have limits to your tolerance. If the behavior of those close to you reaches your limits of tolerance, carefully and caringly let them know those limits. If they persist in exceeding those limits, consider what it is doing to your emotional health and consequently your physical health. Firmly but caringly take a stand. Persist if necessary.

You have likely read and heard this many times. *Be your best friend.* Take care of yourself. If someone's behavior is testing the limit of your tolerance, you may conclude that it is time to let him know. Everyone has limits. If you cannot bring yourself to tell him, it may be advisable to seek help. In childhood you may have been trapped in such situations, but not now. No one is making you stay in an unhealthy situation. You stay because you do not feel good about your belief regarding consequences of leaving. Unfortunately, at times you may not have an easy or acceptable alternative.

Let others know your likes and dislikes. If others *want* to, and are able and willing to demonstrate respect for your desires, they will stop behaving in ways that stress you. You can then feel better and be able to be and do more for others.

The aged manipulative parent may be expert in manipulating the adult child. Guilt trips are commonly imposed. If one is a victim of manipulation, he must start taking care of number one. If he does not, he allows himself to be dragged down. If it continues long enough, it will prevent him from doing well for those whom he loves. It surely will shorten his life. He must take charge in a firm but caring way, and set limits. He need not feel guilty. Anyone who loves him will not knowingly endanger his health. But how can one know another's desires and limits if he is not told?

Allowing oneself to be manipulated detrimentally by a friend or an elderly parent is *not* an act of honor or respect for either. Setting firm limits with a loved one is not reducing love or showing disrespect. It is done for health's sake. It is taking care of oneself so that he can be more to others including his parents. He will feel better while living longer.

SCENARIO. Sally's good friend, Debbie, has lost her husband and is lonely and feeling sorry for herself. Debbie has a severe need to talk about her troubles. She has been calling Sally several times a day for weeks. She is seriously interfering with Sally's job and home life. For her health's sake, Sally must draw lines. "Debbie, I want to hear from you, but I've been spending too much time on the phone. I have so many things to do. Our friendship is important to me but I have to take care of my job and my family. Please try to understand. I hope you *can.* The best time for you to call me is two or three times a week early in the evenings. I hope this will be OK with you."

If Debbie persists in unreasonable calls or visits, Sally must be firm. Her health is at stake. "I care for you very much, Debbie, but I cannot continue taking so much time away from my work and family. I value your friendship but you persist in calling me too often. I just can't take that much time to talk. I have a lot of work to do. Deb, except in a real emergency and your early evening calls, please wait for me to call you. I promise I'll call when I can find the time. I know you get lonely. There are support groups you can join. If you get to know a few more people and make some more friends, you'll feel a lot better. I may be able to call only once or twice a week but it is going to have to be that way. I love you, but I can't handle it any other way."

If Debbie continues in her attempts, Sally must also persist and not hesitate to carefully and caringly repeat the same words and sentences. If Debbie feels free to persist in her repetition, so can Sally. If Sally believes she spoke clearly the first time, she can use the same words and sentences again. But there is a limit to that also. If repeated messages do not have an effect, an answering machine or phone number ID can be used to screen calls even though Debbie *knows* the calls are being screened. Dependency is not love. Sally need not feel guilty. It is her mind, her body, her health, her future and the future of her family at stake. And if one's mind and body are troubled, so is faith in any *thing* or any *one*.

If you find yourself being manipulated, what are you allowing to happen? Check your body for stress. Check your stomach, your shoulders, your hands, your throat. Again, what are you allowing to happen to yourself? You are not honoring or showing respect for another by allowing anyone to stress you, to make you ill, to shorten your life, and to get in the way of your faith. Are you thinking, "But,...?" If you are being manipulated, your health is at risk.

You may find yourself trapped in manipulative situations such as being in a job with an unreasonable boss, or in what may have become a nearly intolerable marriage. Do your best to resolve the problems through understanding. If that fails, no one *makes* you stay. However, think in terms of probable long and short-range consequences of staying or leaving. Which consequences are most desirable?

There is no substitute for carefully and caringly teaching others how you want to be treated. Teach them your likes, dislikes, and limits. How else can they know how you want them to treat you? The Golden Rule does not get the job done. It states, "Do unto others as you would have them do unto you." Some want to be led. Others not. Some want to make decisions. Others not. A masochist wants to be physically punished. I do not. If you only hint at likes and dislikes, the risk of being misunderstood is too great. One has enough difficulty being understood when writing or speaking as plainly as he can.

What if it is the *other* person that wants to get out of the relationship? You may believe you *love* that person, but what *is* it that you love? Behavior? Philosophical views that will never become manifest? A body? Sexual activity? Fantasies? Wishes? Promises? A needed companion? Unrealistic dreams? Hoped-for security? Do you feel dependent? Is the other dependent?

If both were in love *once*, you *still are*. Love is unconditional. It is not negotiable. It cannot be turned on and off like a light. It does not erode away because of arguments or offenses. If it ever existed, it still does. But *was it love*? *Is it love*?

Make a list of the other's personal attributes and behaviors as they really *are*, not as you *want* them to be. Dependency is not love. Domination is not love. Sex is not love. Do you really love that person, or is it something else, a need, or *mutual* needs?

Communications

An incessant talker may give an impression that he is making himself known to you. He may even believe it. But does he really disclose of himself? Do you really know what he is like inside? *What* is he communicating? He may speak of his work, of things, places, hobbies, happenings, successes, and without once disclosing of himself.

Thoreau said it takes two to communicate the truth - one to speak it, the other to hear it. Bias and prejudice may prevent the accuracy of either. Some hear only words, not thoughts. Words are heard, merely by being present. Hearing the *substance* of one's words, hearing another's *thoughts* requires *sustained interested attention of the listener*. However, *both* need the opportunity to question and explain.

Silence can shout, but there is nothing wrong with a few moments of silence. When you are with another or in a group, it is not necessary for someone always to be talking. There is nothing wrong with just thinking.

Morality

What is morality? What is moral? Neither statistics nor majority opinion can be the basis for determining morality or right. Society listens to, reads, and may act on suggestions of the articulate. They may or may not be moral.

Morality has to do with what is good for humanity now and in the future. And what if everyone were to behave in that same manner? What is important for the welfare of self, society, the nation, and the world? Who is to say? Who is the authority? Who has the intelligence and wisdom to judge the actions of another? Yet to a degree, a parent *must* judge. If he does not, who *will*? His friends? Gangs? Congress? The President? If he does not base his decisions on morality, on what?

Author and psychologist, Tomatsu Shibutani wrote:

> In the last analysis, human society rests upon the personal obligations that people feel toward one another.... Moral conduct consists of behavior that has no other sanction than the actor's own sense of right and wrong.[1]

The last sentence above is perhaps very accurate in its

---

[1] Shibutani, Tomatsu. Society and Personality. Prentice Hall. Englewood Cliffs.

portrayal of how morality *is* sanctioned in most societies, *but* that does *not* denote correctness or desirability. The emotionally *unhealthy and immoral* also give or withhold sanction, as do the emotionally *healthy and moral*. It is important to realize who is doing the sanctioning. Persons with deviant behavior may ridicule or misinterpret Judeo-Christian values and writings in order to justify their aberrant behavior in the hope that society will sanction their behavior as moral. Unfortunately many *do* and *will*. Politicians weasel-word their speeches and answers in an attempt to avoid being held accountable. Bankers renew loans that are known candidates for default to avoid carrying them as bad loans. Companies reorganize to obscure audit trails and accountability. Who is doing the sanctioning? Politicians and those who vote for them, and highly respected Chief Executive Officers of respected corporations and those who vote for Board members who appoint the CEOs.

One of the more difficult areas of discussion with a child is that of morality. In those things that are moral, a child needs encouragement to try to exceed what he believes are his limits. He cannot know limits until he tries and fails. Failing does not make him a failure. He needs to be taught.

What is deemed moral in one nation may be immoral and unacceptable in another nation or culture. Before one passes judgment as to right and wrong, good and evil, he must first consider the quality of consequences to humanity, now and later.

Those on a quest for election or reelection to public office may be more interested in votes than in morality of legislation. The result is that some questionable behaviors are sanctioned or overlooked, and even financially supported by various levels of government.

Each person has his own sense of right and wrong, but desirably, each will decide on acceptable standards that he believes to be and are good for humanity. Love for humanity demands morality. Morality demands love. One must think in terms of consequences to humanity and make his views known to others for their consideration.

What effect will actions have now, tomorrow, and next year, in our culture, in our nation, in the world, and on future generations? Is the nation to let standards of morality be set by other nations, the courts, attorneys, deviants, congress, the president, politicians, illegal immigrants, the news media, the entertainment media, or street gangs? Each of them has a sense of right and wrong. You have yours. I have mine. We, all of society collectively, have *ours*. The course we are pursuing is questionable at best. Views of morality change. A few prayers for wisdom and guidance wouldn't hurt.

Chapter 9
SURVIVING THE WORKPLACE

Fun Place or Stress Place?

What does the workplace have to do with all of this? A lot. Perceived offenses abound in the workplace, some misperceived. The offended are stressed. Stress kills. Increased understanding of the workplace and its participants and problems leads to forgiveness. *Forgiveness is a critically important step in resolving the negative emotions that cause the stress.*

Most adults of working age are employed or self-employed. The workplace can be an inspirational and a fun-place, or it can be frustrating and a stress-place. Stress affects mental and physical health of owners, executives, and subordinate employees, plus it indirectly and individually affects all others who are significant to each of them.

Long hours are spent in the workplace and in traveling to and from it. Many take work home. Many spend a lot of time thinking about work while driving to and from work, and while eating, playing, and trying to sleep. Anyone in the workplace may have a direct role in contributing to the stress of employees, managers, executives, and *indirectly* to the stress of their significant others outside the workplace.

Much of what is important in the workplace is also important to the family system and its relationships. Emotions are carried from the workplace into the home and from the home back into the workplace. They are carried into social life. They affect families, friends, and all levels of employees.

A non-working mother is not a part of the workplace, however it is likely that a spouse, or one or more persons significant to her, plays a role in it. She may likely feel the stress of the workplace. Her spouse may carry her second-hand stress and *different* emotions *back into* the workplace. An understanding of managers, subordinates, and their peer relationships will contribute toward a healthier life for her and consequently the family.

Persons at every level within an organization are affected. Managers stress employees. Employees stress managers. Managers stress each other. Employees stress each other. Although stress is generally thought of as being imposed by external sources, it is *self-imposed* and felt as a result of one's own unconscious beliefs.

To feel better, each person in the workplace will benefit from understanding the problems of peers, associates, subordinates, and superiors. Employees at all levels need to understand what each can contribute to improving the work environment. The workplace environment affects lives during and after work, even after retirement. The emotions may linger on in a family even after the employee's death.

Employees may work a full shift and considerably more overtime than they want. Some do not like the consequences of refusing. Others work only part-time and are desperate for full-time work. Some are anxiously facing possible termination of their jobs. Many feel critical both of peers and management. Some are jealous of other employees. Unresolved, the feelings may turn to anger. In performing assignments, one may advisedly *avoid* viewing a task as being in *competition* with his peers. He may better compete against his own standards, his own record of accomplishments. This allows for more enjoyable working relationships with his peers.

A recent survey determined that heart attacks occur at the highest frequency approximately 9:00 AM on Monday mornings. Workers may feel weary merely through associative recall of physical feelings. They are predisposed to expect, "Another hard day at the office. I'm facing another whole week of this. I'm back at the salt mine." Merely entering the work environment associatively recalls last week's stress, and weeks before that.

Many in the workplace feel fear, frustration, anger, or disgust. They may feel trapped in an unchanging work environment. They would like to effect change and may have tried without success. Old feelings of helplessness may rise. Many feel unrecognized and underpaid. They feel they are treated unfairly. Many hold their emotions inside. They feel pressured.

132

A European study of 2000 people concluded that those who hold back emotions and fail to resolve their problems of stress are more likely to get cancer and heart disease. However, the workplace is not an appropriate place to freely vent emotions. Another study showed that stressed persons catch colds more easily.

Is the Manager Managing?

A stressed manager or top executive stresses subordinates and peers. A manager may be incompetent. Subordinates may be severely stressed by awareness of mismanagement of "*our company.*"

Why should a top executive feel stressed? He may be working an excessive number of hours on a sustained basis. He is stressing himself whether or not he recognizes the fact. With many managers, questions may be in order. They may assist an employee in deciding whether or not he wants to remain with an organization. Following are only a few of the more than 300 questions that I *could* ask of a manager or top executive.

Is he requiring and conducting substantive and timely briefings? Does he hold unnecessary or untimely meetings? Does he schedule the start time and duration of meetings to enable subordinates to schedule *their* time? Does he make known his meeting agenda? Does he keep subordinates informed?

Is he periodically briefed on exceptions, and on subordinates' problems and plans? Does he follow-up to assure action? Are written procedures required and kept current for all functions? If not, how do supervisors know what they are supervising? In nearly every work group I have analyzed, subordinates performed functions of which supervision was not even aware. Does the company audit its procedures or engage procedural auditors? If not, who is assuring that procedures are followed? Are efforts being duplicated?

If he has a sales staff, does he require weekly sales plans and sales reports? If not, how does he know how they are spending their time? What does he believe he is managing? Has he hired sales persons or are they just order-takers?

Is he training his replacement? Does he have written and distributed delegations of authority? Before he leaves on a trip, does he designate an acting manager, and make it known? Does he have a schedule for subordinates' budget submission, review, and approval? Was *his* requested budget approved? If the budget was approved, is he properly staffed? If he is properly staffed, why is he not delegating the work where it belongs? Or does he not trust his subordinates? If he has delegated properly, why is he working late and on weekends? Did he select incompetent subordinates, or is he mismanaging? Why is he not generally completing his work in an eight-hour day? Is he in over his head? If he is, does he realize it? Incompetent management is a source of stress to all.

Unfortunately, *circumstance* may dictate longer working hours for the *best* of managers. If his superiors make incompetent or self-serving budget and bottom-line decisions, he may become understaffed or overloaded with work. He may be facing an inordinate number of decisions requiring analysis. If so, has he required well-researched and well-organized decision papers from subordinates? This can take a number of the monkeys off his back and reduce the downward pressure on subordinates.

Modern computer printers can turn out pages faster than the eye can follow. This is not reason to require micro-management reports. Has the manager stated his requirements for the development of exception-report screens that identify areas needing his attention? Computers were predicted to reduce paperwork, yet office paper sales have more than doubled in the past few years. This must say something about management.

A workaholic manager may have unrealistic expectations of subordinates. He may be projecting his own dedications or needs to subordinates. They may have different and *personal* goals and objectives. They feel unfairly pressured over having to work with the boss through lunch hours, into the night, and on weekends to meet his expectations.

Do I Want to Work Here?

If an employee is a low performer, it is *not* appropriate to ignore him in meetings or while walking down a hallway, or in a parking area. Ignoring him attributes a value of *zero* to him. It *is* appropriate to *deal* with the problem, but in the *office*. There is no substitute for speaking clearly and carefully about the problems and possible resolutions. A manager may not be able to *give* employees dignity, but he *can let* them retain what they *have*.

Is he retaining a low performer? Why? He would possibly be doing him a favor by terminating him. An employee may be in the wrong job, one for which he is not qualified. The sooner he moves into a career field that matches his skills, knowledge, abilities, and personal attributes, the better off he will be, and the better off the organization will be.

The current trend is toward leaderless and near-leaderless teams. Many employees may not have such an invitation or opportunity, if it *is* an opportunity. Teams need qualified leaders to hold employees accountable and to fairly allocate recognition, awards, and rewards for individuals' contributions to the group's accomplishments.

Teamwork is essential for efficiency, but in work assignments, who is accountable if the direction is, "You guys do it?" Who is going to assure that the team efforts are directed toward meeting stated organizational objectives? And what if there are two outstanding performers in a team of 10 that fails to meet goals? Eight of them may be *fearful* because of the *group failure*. Two of them may be *angry* because of *management methods*. If no one is officially in charge, who is going to evaluate individual performance? Suppose the team *does* fail. If the two high performers do not get recognition, will the manager expect those high performers to stay? If individual excellence is not recognized, is he prepared for an exodus of high performers? He can expect them to leave at first opportunity, perhaps at an inopportune time for the organization. *Good supervision and team spirit are not mutually exclusive.*

Employees want to know that an organization is efficient and fair. If management does not designate a leader in a group effort, a leader *will arise*. He may not be the best. He may not be qualified. If a leader is not designated, too often it is the loudly articulate, sharp elbowed, and rude that push to the front. Many have become articulate from having spent a great deal of their working hours talking instead of working. They also get practice speaking comfortably because they do not hold themselves accountable for what they are saying. Other employees, deeply and usually without management's knowledge, resent management's approval or unawareness of such assumption of control. Outstanding employees have their opinions on leaderless teams.

Does the boss tolerate liars? If an employee is a liar, what *else* is he? As a child, I trusted everyone. I was raised in a small town in an environment of trust. We would leave town for a week leaving all doors unlocked. My parents did not even possess keys to the locks on the doors of our home. I still have the tendency to trust. Any manager may have the same tendency. However he owes it to the organization to establish effective controls over all resources and significant transactions, including computer games and Internet access.

Personal economic pressure may make liars, cheats, and thieves out of otherwise honest people. The store needs watching. Expectations of honesty should be made common knowledge. It is advisable to think twice before giving an employee a second chance at honesty. Honesty is one of the most critical attributes in business. How can one do business with liars, cheats, or thieves within or outside the organization? If dishonesty is tolerated, it may spread. The negative consequences may be boundless.

Schooling and Training

Some studies show that young persons entering the job market will change jobs an average of seven or eight times during their working careers. These numbers will increase. Changes may occur without leaving an organization. Because of rapid change, knowledge and skills may quickly become obsolete. Retraining or upgrading of skills and knowledge will be required throughout a career. Middle-aged employees are prone to say, "I'm too old to go back to school. I'm too old to learn something new." Upper management often has the same belief about subordinates, in some cases irrespective of their own advanced ages.

I am not seeking and do not need anyone's approbation. I am only trying to make a point. Irrespective of age, you need not fear schooling or training. No one is ever too old to learn. After attending night school for each degree, I received a bachelor's degree in business technology, summa cum laude, at age 51, a master's at age 52, and a second master's at age 64. I received a Ph.D. in clinical psychology at age 66. Until I was seated next to another senior citizen at graduation, I thought I would be, by decades, the oldest doctoral candidate at graduation. During a pause in the ceremony, I turned to speak with him. He was 68.

If you are being left out of the schooling and training loop, request both. If all else fails, undertake at least *some* outside schooling on your own to prove desire and ability.

Training is important to an organization, but is effective only if learned skills and knowledge are used. Unused knowledge is worthless. If employees have attended training sessions, formal or otherwise, and are not assigned work involving the knowledge, they will lose much of it. Employees recognize waste. They wonder about management that approved the waste of the two basic resources, time and money. Perceived waste stresses efficient and loyal employees. Loyalty wanes.

Precaution

The following may be of serious importance to an employee who is considering taking a perceived problem to management. Taking a problem to the boss *will result* in his *taking action*. It may be in a different direction and to a greater degree than the subordinate desired. He has placed his boss in a position of having to follow up with investigation and action. If one escalates a problem, the boss simply *cannot risk ignoring it*. The cost of the boss' time is highly leveraged. He has none to waste.

His job is always on the line. If the allegation is found to be factually *unsupported*, he may think, "How *dare* you put my job at risk?" Is he stressed? Is he indignant? A *bunch*.

One must not allow desire for recognition or promotion to drive him to foolish efforts to try to impress the boss. Before presenting problems to management, one can determine that the problem factually exists. He can learn as much about the problem as time reasonably allows before he presents it. A Decision Paper (Appendix D) may be an aid in doing so. If you are in such a situation, go through the drill of creating one. Write it as though you are going to submit it. It will help decide if an idea is worth submitting. If you determine it *is* worthy, submit it. However, your boss may take the credit, and it may be the first decision paper he has ever seen.

Dedication

If one allows himself only one unnecessary absence from his job, who will do his work? Management understands emergencies and scheduled vacations, but has very low tolerance for truancy or tardiness by an employee who feels compelled to attend the races or watch the World Series. Tardiness or unauthorized absences stress the employee, his peers who have to do his work, and his manager. Road repair, inclement weather, and other circumstances will slow driving or riding. This requires leaving for work earlier than usual. Arrival on time is an expectation of management. Even *valid* exceptions are expected to be rare. Grabbing at weak excuses to be late or to take unauthorized time off may result in an involuntary job change. Deception is much the same as lying. The boss does not easily forget being stressed. "If *you* don't care about *me and the organization*, why should I care about *you*?"

Generally an employee is evaluated and compensated within a pay scale based on the sustained quality, quantity, and timeliness of his work. However, the boss also evaluates him off the record from a somewhat subjective viewpoint. "How difficult or how easy are you making it for me to do my job?" Resist challenging your boss in front of others. If he is an autocrat, *never* challenge him.

Dedicated and well-coordinated workers on production lines may have performance rates that exceed expectations by as much as 50%, perhaps even 100%. However some of our high tech jobs are dependent more on mental capability and the motivation to use it. A brilliant hi-tech employee may be able to outperform the average of the others by *1000 per cent*. Performance at such a level simply does not fit anywhere in organizational pay schedules. It is likely not conceivable to salary and pay administrators. The compensation of these very exceptional employees is rarely if ever commensurate with benefit to the organization.

However, a job applicant agrees on his compensation when he accepts the job. His acceptance implies that he will give the job his best effort during *all* of his assigned working hours. Management may become well aware of his unusual capabilities and his accomplishments. Regardless of his inordinate capabilities, management expects him to work at his full capacity, to be a role model. If as a role model he wastes time, what is to be expected of co-workers? "Me too."

This very capable employee may complete the equivalent of an average employee's entire day's work in a very brief time, perhaps in one hour. He may spend the rest of the day talking to and interfering with other employee's efforts. Total work accomplished may be less than if he were not there at all. No competent manager will tolerate it.

Understand the Boss

Merely *being* in disagreement with a manager's decision may stress a subordinate. Perhaps more so if that subordinate is loyal to the company and because he wants the company to do and be at its best. Well-thought-out suggestions, along with creative and precautionary thinking, should be brought to management's attention in an appropriate manner and at an appropriate time, and only once. If one presents his ideas again after they have been rejected, is he not being argumentative? "Don't beat a dead horse."

Someone must be in charge. The *boss* is in charge. He makes the decisions, right or wrong. Each manager has beliefs and feelings regarding management style and decisions. A subordinate's are sometimes different. He may suggest change. A qualified subordinate's one-time suggestion may and should be welcomed by his manager, but even if it is, he may not be able to change the manager's thinking and feeling. Any subsequent suggestion to make the same change will likely not ever be acceptable to the manager. Why?

IMAGINE. The boss has made a decision. He *feels* it is the right decision. Based on briefings by others, analysis of the available data, and his intuition, he has settled on *the* decision about which he felt, and likely still *feels the best*. He felt and still feels less than enthused when thinking about the *other* choices. If a subordinate were to come to him suggesting his own different idea, is the boss likely to implement it unless it is better *with certainty*? He would have to retract his first decision. He would be admitting to all that he made a mistake. He could not feel good doing so. Would anyone knowingly make or change a decision, or take an action that is going to make him feel miserable? Would a wise employee repeatedly go to his manager and say, "Do it my way instead so that you can feel *distressed*?"

If one persists in pushing ideas that the boss does not like, he risks his job. He is insisting that the boss admit his error and feel miserable. The boss does not *want* to implement decisions that conflict with his own. That is another circumstance in an employee's life. The same thinking applies to suggesting change in long-standing procedures. The boss has not chosen to change them. The implication is that the boss believes those procedures are OK.

A manager may persist in the pursuit of a continuously and unrealistically higher production rate. He has a longer way to fall than his subordinates do. His standard of living may be higher. He may have more difficulty finding another job. He may require completion of an assignment in an unrealistic length of time. He may have been given an unrealistic objective by higher management. He is feeling pressured. He is afraid to tell higher management that the goal is unachievable in the time allowed.

140

He fears failure. Instead of facing up to his boss, he passes the pressure on to subordinates with mandates and perhaps with veiled and hollow threats.

The pendulum syndrome is best avoided. It is over-reaction to higher-level directives, suggestions, or comments. Jumping too soon too far, before knowing what end results are expected and made clearly known, may cause subordinates to overreact to already over-amplified CEO requests that may have been intended *merely for consideration by subordinates*. If the pendulum swings too far and one wonders why, look to the hierarchy of management. No one has broken the chain of fear. No one has dared. Each has chosen to be politically correct.

However, It is important to be aware that a manager has sources of information that subordinates do not have. He has more visibility. He has a broader view of the total organization. He may not be able to share his information for a variety of reasons. He may have plans that he cannot discuss. He may have been subjected to demands of which subordinates may be totally unaware. The manager sees a bigger picture not available to subordinates. A decision may seem wrong to uninformed subordinates, but when all facts are made known, it may be an excellent decision.

On the other hand, if one's manager is widely considered incompetent, one may want to look for another job within the same organization. He may wonder why top management is tolerating an incompetent manager. Or is the problem a larger one? Is the organization mismanaged as a whole? There are consequences to leaving. There are consequences to staying. There are tradeoffs.

No one *makes* an employee do anything. No one is holding a gun to his head. No one *makes* him carry out management directives. No one *physically twists his arm*. He does have a choice. He has a choice is to leave or stay, but before that decision is made, *consequences* are to be *carefully considered*, well thought out.

A subordinate may believe that his job is threatened by an unreasonable superior. It is more likely that the threat stems from the manager's feelings of desperation, and is not meant at all. It is rather a reaction to his own unfounded fears of higher management. He fearfully hopes that his mandates and downward pressure will somehow accelerate the work process. If one feels pressured at work, he needs the following philosophical view. *I am able to do only what I am able to do regardless of mandates from above, and if that is not good enough, I shall let it be the manager's problem.*

Unless one can accurately and with certainty forecast the future, why forecast anything negative? Robert Schuller's, *No one knows enough to be pessimistic* is worthy of being posted on the bathroom mirror.

A competent employee may be *able* to withstand attempted pressure very well, but he may choose *not* to. He may be confident of his performance abilities and of his job retention. He may be immune to unreasonable demands. The pressure-plays may merely aggravate him. He may decide to terminate his job simply out of *disgust* with the organization. Although disgust is an emotion and it drives his behavior, his decision to leave *is logical*. Enough is enough. Unless he is retiring, it may be wise to first find another job and to get written commitment from his future employer before giving notice to his present employer.

Manage? Who? *Me?*

The best worker may not qualify as a manager. High performers may get promoted into management and fail. Gathering all data related to a decision is rarely possible. Intuition must play a role in the decision-making process. Not everyone makes good intuitive decisions. Intuition is a composite of all associated feelings, and all unconsciously stored knowledge and beliefs that are related to the problem and the desire to solve it. Intuition can cause indecision, bad decisions, or good decisions. If one's intuition treats him badly, his boss may have recognized this. He may not be selected for promotion into management, or if he is already a manager, he may not be promoted.

Not all supervisors are competent. Many employees feel bottlenecked by incompetent supervision. With reading and study, a good student can learn in spite of a poor instructor. Well-managed organizations will have well-documented procedures. With these, and with an inquisitive approach, a good employee can succeed and be promoted into management in spite of poor supervision. If one is in such a situation, a myriad of questions to others may speed learning. He can learn all the whos, whats, what nots, hows, whys, whens, wheres, and what ifs. It is appropriate to seek the information at appropriate times and in appropriate places, but *not* at the expense of current performance. Well-documented procedures also accelerate and improve training of new employees.

Today, one may have no interest in becoming a manager. "*Never say never.*" He may one day change his mind. His belief system is constantly evolving. Tomorrow may be the breakpoint when he suddenly decides he wants to manage.

One Manager's Viewpoints

Based on comments made by managers after a long-ago seminar, other managers and their subordinates may benefit from considering the following. [1]

❏ There is no substitute for honesty.
❏ Quality can happen only with sustained support from the top.
❏ Exchange expectations with your employees.
❏ Circumstance can make a procrastinator wish he hadn't.
❏ If it doesn't contribute to objectives, don't do it.
❏ The mechanics of management control are simple. People are not.
❏ You cannot do more than you are able to do. If that is not good enough, consider making plans to leave.
❏ None of authoritative denials, delegations of authority, absences, implied finger- pointing, buck passing, nor closed doors can rid a manager of responsibility.
❏ A womanager is as good as a manager.

---

[1] From a paper presented at a management seminar.
© Copyright 1984 Howard Otterholt.

- Manage your in-basket or it will manage you.
- Someone else's good fortune is not your good fortune and conversely.
- One does not live long enough to get *all* the facts for making any major decision.
- If your intuition treats you badly, stay out of top management.
- When evaluating a subordinate's comments or answers, distinguish between pessimism and realism.
- Hold your yes-men accountable. (I had thoughtlessly omitted *yes-women*.)
- If you do not follow-up and hold subordinates accountable, you are not in control.
- Avoid promoting or commending before accomplishments have been measured, or effectiveness determined.
- Undue pressure promotes dishonesty, fear, and exodus.
- Forgiveness contributes to objectivity and health.
- Recognition and acceptance of uncontrollable circumstance also contribute to objectivity and health.
- In a world of change, organizations need conformity, shared creativity, and teamwork.
- Know what it is for which you are giving recognition. Those who are unrecognized may wonder.
- A high IQ test score indicates the ability to rapidly do a lot of little things well for a short period of time.
- Reorganizations tend to break audit trails and lose accountability.
- Undocumented current procedures are reason to wonder if and what management is controlling.
- Read. Listen. Consider. Accept or reject.
- Communicate carefully and caringly. Misunderstanding breeds.
- As you come to understand others, do not expect understanding from them.
- Ignoring someone attributes a value of zero to that person.
- Work at letting others retain dignity.
- Take the time to teach others how to treat you.
- If something needs saying, say it.

- Forgiveness leads to better perception, clearer analysis, and better choices for yourself and those about whom you care.
- The world is in constant change. You and your organization are relative to all else. Define. Analyze. Decide. Conceptualize. Design. Plan. Strategize. Develop. Implement. Operate. Monitor. Modify. Have a voice in your changes.
- All decisions have consequences wherein morality is an important consideration.
- Documented delegations of chain-of-command authority limit and allow. Undocumented delegations do neither very well.

What Now?

Many of my prior subordinates, most very intelligent and some tested as genius, including managers and hi-tech employees, commented that they were bored with work, and wondered how they could find challenge and interest. My answer was nearly always the same.

There is more to life than work. Excitement, challenge, and spiritual and psychological growth may have to come from outside the workplace. No matter what your vocation, look outside the workplace for nurturing and psychological growth. You may find it among, family, friends, relatives, churches, and various groups. You may find it in accomplishment outside the workplace, especially in doing for others. You may benefit from involvement in sports, hobbies and crafts, volunteer work, school, church, reading, and learning. There *is a life after work.* It can be found if one seeks it.

Chapter 10
OUT OF THE PAST

The Closet of Your Mind

This chapter consists mainly of abstracts of hypnotherapy sessions that are presented in the hope that they will be read with more than just interest. If they are read carefully they serve as evidence of the benefit of understanding the process of childhood beginnings of desires, beliefs, and emotions.

Unfortunately, merely hearing or reading the term hypnosis may elicit feelings of discomfort, fear, or contempt. Some believe that hypnosis is faked. Many have been conditioned by hearsay, misinformed news media, unrealistic and overly imaginative moviemakers, or misinterpretation of and oversight in literature, both religious and otherwise. I am a Christian. I encounter many Christians who seem appalled that anyone would undergo hypnosis. All hypnosis is self-hypnosis. The state of hypnosis is commonly called the trance state. The Apostles, Peter and Paul, prayed in the trance state. Acts 10:10, Acts 11:5, and Acts 22:17. Also, check Numbers 24:4 and 24:16. For another, "But thou, when thou prayest, enter into thy closet." (Matt 6:6) I believe Jesus was referring to the unconscious mind, certainly not a clothes or broom closet.

The hypnotic state is an altered state of consciousness in which one places himself many times each day. A person who is reading while at the same time seemingly engaged in a conversation, and at times not hearing the other, is in such a state. A child intently watching TV, and not hearing his name when it is spoken, is in a trance state. An automobile driver who is surprised that he has just driven past his freeway turnoff, or suddenly realizes he has arrived at his destination, has been in such a state.

The following therapy abstracts are presented to serve as evidence that we are driven and inhibited by what we have stored in the unconscious from earlier times. Clients experiencing hypnosis were able to regress to the childhood causative experiences that began the development of desires, beliefs, and emotions that carried into adulthood.

They came to realize that they themselves were not to be blamed for having developed their own negative beliefs and desires, or for their anger, fear, frustration, helplessness, plus a host of other negative feelings. They came to realize that it is only logical that their offenders, *too*, could not be blamed for having developed negative beliefs and feelings by which they were unconsciously controlled, and therefore were and are worthy of forgiveness. They, as with everyone else, were victims of the sins of the fathers. Believed understanding of this is the only path I know to genuine forgiveness, to feeling good, to being able to love others, and to freely making healthy and moral choices.

I performed original research in hypnosis for two postgraduate degrees. I may never otherwise have started down the road of learning what I have been writing. My beliefs were later reinforced by having observed the causes, results, and ultimate changes in hundreds of clients. Case results served as assured evidence to me that understanding and forgiveness are essential to mental, physical, and spiritual health.

Effects of So-called Prior Lives

As you read the abstracts you will note that some clients appeared to regress to what may be thought to be a prior life. A so-called prior-life's feelings and experiences may be unconsciously associated with today's troublesome emotions. Memories are recalled and felt as though the client had lived that life. It is not my intent to debate the subject of reincarnation. However, as a matter of reader interest, it is possible, through unconscious mental telepathy, for those feelings and memories of events to have been passed down over many decades and centuries, from generation to generation and half way around the world. The mind is very fast and easily capable of accepting the memories of hundreds of the "other life's" experiences in moments. Further, Scripture tells us that it is appointed unto men once to die (Heb 9:27). Irrespective of the source of the seemed

148

memories, if they are negative, they must be resolved.

Case History Abstracts

This chapter is made up primarily of abstracts of therapy notes. Please keep in mind that each client's coming to awareness of the experiences, coupled with a believed understanding and forgiveness of offenders, is essential to cure. One experience may recall another, not necessarily in original sequence. It is the momentary levels of feelings regarding events that determine which memory will next be recalled. Careful reading of the abstracts may increase understanding of the genesis of unconsciously stored emotions, beliefs, and unfulfilled desires, and how they become reinforced through subsequent experiences. Some causes of the symptoms may be obvious. Explanations of some were deemed necessary.

Each client's symptoms are listed at the beginning of the abstract. Their comments and responses will be of more interest if you keep the symptoms in mind as you read. Some abstracts end abruptly. Those clients suddenly believed that no further work was needed.

Indicators in the abstracts: (OK to skip and refer back if necessary.)

- Suggestions, comments, and questions to the client are enclosed in parentheses ( ).
- Explanations to the reader are in brackets [ ].
- Significant time lapses of various lengths are shown by a series of dots .... .
- Hesitation is represented by a dash - .
- A triple asterisk *** marks the *beginning* of the recall of an event.
- Abstracts are divided into paragraphs only for ease in reading.

Abstracts

MALE, LATE 30s, ANXIETY, HESITANT
SPEECH, FEAR OF CRITICISM,
AND LOW SELF-ESTEEM.

REMINDER: Triple asterisks [***] designate the beginning of each event in the sequence in which it was being recalled.

*** I'm at work. Difficulty talking with boss. *** Messing my pants. My mother said it's stupid. *** In playground. Have a basketball. Not good at dribbling or shooting. Out of breath. Tired. Always get tired. High School. Running hurdles. If I didn't do this, I would be ridiculed. *** School band class. I really couldn't play the instrument. Teacher berated me. *** Kindergarten. Made a painting. Too much yellow.

*** Playing with matches in grandparents' back yard. Started a fire. I ran over to the swing and pretended I didn't know anything about it. Dad asked me and I lied to protect myself. *** Don't want to get beaten - I don't know why I'm going to be beaten. *** Going to see movie with friends. They got in but I didn't. The line got cut off at me. *** Playing basketball. I threw a pass through a window. Felt like crying but couldn't.

*** With a Jr. High group at car wash. Squeegee broke window. I didn't do anything wrong. Wanted to cry but couldn't. *** Walked in my sleep. Peed in the gas heater. Thought it was the bathroom. Going to be criticized. *** In church. I asked a man how he got in a wheel chair. My mother said I'm not supposed to ask questions. *** Grandmother is oil painting. I made a small painting. My mother was very critical.

After realizing the causes of his feelings, and after understanding and forgiving the too critical adults, he was rid of the feelings of inadequacy and low self-esteem.

FEMALE, MID 60s
ANGER TOWARD DECEASED FATHER

*** With my mother. I'm 3. My father is not part of my life.
*** I'm 3. I think I have been sexually assaulted. My vagina

hurts. I wonder if someone put stones up there. *** I'm 6. My sister is 3 1/2. We're in bed. My brothers are on top of us. It's wrong but it feels good. Now I'm sitting behind the stove. My mother comes in. I'm mad at her for leaving us alone. That's why it happened.

*** I'm sitting outside my father's bedroom window where he is sleeping. Listening for him to wake up. Been drinking. I'm waiting so that I can run and tell my mother he's awake. I'm guarding. I'm making a pact with God that if God will take him, I'll go to church every day for the rest of my life.

*** I'm 3. I'm holding my mother's hand. I feel the same. I'm aware of the smarting in my vagina. *** I'm 3 1/2. My mother is being taken out of the house. People all around. She's holding her arm. Taking her away. A lady says, "You're coming to stay with me." I like that. Everything is in order - clean and peaceful. [Likely a foster home.]

Anger developed over sexual abuse, and at her mother for not protecting her. Emotions toward her father were painful enough that she had wanted him dead. She was able to forgive every family member including her father. Her anger was resolved.

FEMALE EARLY 40s
SEXUAL DYSFUNCTION AND ANXIETY

*** I feel put down - my dad. I'm responsible for his behavior. He is saying I'm bad. I bit him. He puts his penis in my mouth. I'm in the bassinet - in diapers. *** _____ [client's husband] is helping me cook. He's telling me what to do. Makes me feel stupid. *** In school - afraid of teachers. They whipped me so I wouldn't act bad. *** Mother lies to my dad so he whips me. *** I'm angry and inadequate. They say ugly things to me. My dad's usually gone. I don't let him bother me so much. I don't want him to go around the corner because I might lose his love. *** My dad - I'm 3. I don't know what he wants me to do. I feel like I'm disappointing him and I want his love. Sometimes I do what he wants because I want his love. Sometimes he makes me do it.

151

She understood her mother's, father's and teachers' compulsive behavior and forgave them. Her anxiety symptoms ended. I did not receive any feedback as to her sexual dysfunction.

FEMALE, LATE 30s, ANXIETY, FEAR OF HEIGHTS, SEXUAL DYSFUNCTION

*** I never know what my parents are going to do. I'm 12. They're crazy. My father's never home. When he is home, my mother won't let me talk to him. I can't wake him up - alcohol. He always has girl friends. No time for me. I feel my parents are dying. Grandfather's always talking about dying. *** My husband is going to have surgery. I feel boxed in. Can't breathe. Feel like a prisoner. Suffocating. *** Going over a bridge to see my girl friend. Can't do it. Steep mountains. *** I was fired from my job.

*** On my honey moon. We're driving. High. Can't stand it. *** I'm afraid of looking out second story. House is in [city]. I'm 10. The house hurts. I was alone a lot. My mom gave me to my grandmother. *** Working for Doctor [name]. He drives me crazy - conceit. *** My mother wants me to move out. I feel disgusted and unwanted. I've always felt that way. My grandmother hates me. Doesn't treat me very well. Ignores me.

*** I'm always having to get married. I'm either sick or having job problems. I get married to escape. I can't breathe. *** I'm afraid of being alone. 6th grade. A girl got the whole class to stop talking to me. *** I'm 5. Started masturbating. It's just that I'm ugly. Everybody says I'm ugly. My sister hates me. My uncle is molesting me. Putting his hands all over me. I'm afraid.

*** In my apartment. Playing a board game with an acquaintance. He raped me. On the floor. Kisses me. I don't want that. He's tearing my clothes off. Fighting. I gave in. *** I'm being robbed - gun. I'm getting out of car. Gun in my stomach. Robbed me. Drives away. *** Afraid of being alone. Always feel alone. Always left out. *** Family is together. I'm standing in the corner. Feel alone. *** I want to be loved. I don't feel loved at home. My parents - my sister. They pay attention to my sister.

After discovering the truth regarding the source of her symptoms, she understood and forgave all of her offenders. All of her symptoms reduced to the point of being negligible.

MALE, LATE THIRTIES, EXTREME ANGER, LOW SELF ESTEEM, SEXUAL DYSFUNCTION, OBESE (380 lbs.)

*** I'm in the womb. My mom is poking me. She's telling me I'm bad for waking her up like that in the night. *** I'm being born - slime. *** Telling me to stop soiling my diapers - Mom. Eat and sh__, eat and sh__. That's all you do. *** In school. I'm getting beat up on. Kids. I'm fat and ugly. They don't want me around. *** Mrs. _____ [name], neighbor lady, showed me what to do with my pee pee. She made my peeper stand up. When I touch her there she makes funny noises. Milk and cookies. *** In the bathroom at school. On the pot. Pants down. The older kids take my pants. I had to sit there all day. I escape into anger.

*** I feel like I'm in a funnel. A nurse did it. She shoved me in a hamper with the used diapers. Crying. Nurse is saying, "Shut up." She piles diapers on me... I'm falling on the floor. A nurse says, "Oh my God. We've got to get him breathing." They punch on my tummy - punch on my tummy - punch on my tummy. I'm with the doctor. This thing on his face. The doctor says, "There. Now he's breathing." Bounces me up and down. They feed me. Now I'm with Mom. *** Feed the dragon. The monster demands it. Daddy talking. He's going to feed me. Powerful ruler of all he sees. When he talks, everyone listens. When he stops, we get to eat. We say grace first.

*** I'm unhappy. A weight on my chest. Somebody is standing on my chest. I want to eat and get big. *** In the hospital. Got weighed. I crawled into a hole. I'm in a container in the center of the room. Wait a minute - it's an incubator. I'm caught in a hand hole - caught in one of the gloves. *** Mommy never pays attention to me. She'd rather have me eat than bother her. Eating gives me something to do that I won't be punished for. *** She's trying to clean my face with her spit on a hanky. Wants to look good for Grandma. She doesn't want to be considered a bad mother. Only when company comes. *** I have to be bigger than my dad so he can't hit me. Dad's teaching me. How to take it like a man. I hold on to the bedpost while he swats me with the razor strap. I thought that bonded us. Something special between us - man to man.

*** A rag is in my mouth. I swallowed part of it. Dad put the rag in my mouth so the neighbors wouldn't hear me scream. I'm not wiggling any more. The light's getting dimmer. I was at the light where dead people go. He's dragging me back. Breathing problem. He squeezed my stomach and pulled the rag out. He says, "See what you made me do?" *** Mom - she shouldn't have done that to me. Took off my diapers and beat my bare little bottom. She's exploring to see how far she can bend me before I break. *** Breast feeding. Mom leans over and just lets me fall into the crib.

This client had been referred to me by a professional who had given up on him. After the above, improvement was significant, but further treatment was indicated. The client did not agree. On termination, client said, "I am not as angry. I treat my customers better. This is the first time in my life that I have felt I deserve to feel good."

FEMALE, EARLY 30s
PANIC FEAR IN AUTOMOBILES AND
SEXUAL DYSFUNCTION.
COULD NOT UNDRESS IN FRONT
OF HER HUSBAND.

Client could not ride in a car that was destined more than one or two miles from her home. Any attempt to do so resulted in severe stomach pains and almost immediate diarrhea. Because of fear of riding in a car, she could not go out to dinner with her husband.

*** I'm 11. I'm riding with my dad on the way to the train station to meet Mom. He took me to dinner tonight. I have to go to the restroom. My stomach really hurts. I can't wait. We're looking for a parking place. I can't stand it. He's letting me out at the front of the station. I'm running. I'm in the ladies' room. I

154

don't have a dime. Can't open the door to the toilet. I'm crawling under the door. I'm stuck. Can't get in or out. Ohhhhh! I messed all over myself. Can't get loose. People are coming. I could die. A lady gets me loose. People all around. I'm all messy. Have to take off all my clothes. They put a blanket around me. Mom came and we're on the way home.

A car ride had led up to the embarrassment. She feared refeeling the experience that she had associated with the car ride and had repressed memories of the experience. Awareness of the cause resolved the problems. Later her husband sent me a note telling how they were enjoying eating out, and that regarding sex, his wife had said, "I feel like I have died and gone to heaven."

FEMALE, EARLY 30s
NARCOLEPSY
[FALLING ASLEEP AT RANDOM TIMES]

*** Mother doesn't like me. She said, "Go away." (Can you forgive her?) No!! ... Mom and Dad are fighting. I'm scared. Sometimes I hate them. They don't take care of me. I can't make them happy. Mother hit me. (Is she very emotional?) What's emotional? She's angry. I must have done something wrong. *** I'm in 6th grade. Unhappy. About everything. My life seems difficult. I want to leave home. Nowhere to go. Lying in bed. Want to stay awake but pressing desire to sleep. Want to sleep. Want to get away. *** 6th grade with my friends but getting sleepy. I want to get away from Mom and Dad. Teacher doesn't like me either. She doesn't like my handwriting. I want to get away. They fight.

Her narcolepsy disorder had taken control whenever she encountered frustration. It was her way of escaping the negative feelings. Awareness and forgiveness resolved the problem.

FEMALE, LATE 50s
ANXIETY, PARENTAL MANIPULATION

*** Nurses' training. I'm crying. I've been criticized for being a way I can't help. *** At my aunt's for Sunday dinner. Mother is reprimanding me for not talking much. She says they will think I'm snobbish. I told her I was just different. She can't understand. Then I start berating myself. *** Mom slapped me. I don't know why. I don't like putting my arms around her. She has a strange odor. *** In Grandma's home. Family reunion. I'm 6. Just a bunch of chatting women. I don't feel affection. All the old aunts slobber all over us. Phony. I don't want to be smothered. All the men are henpecked. I don't want to be like any of the women and I can't stand the men for letting the women treat them that way.

*** I don't like color blue. *** Blue apron. Mom. I'm crying. She's berating me. Dark blue. Dots. Trimmed in blue bias tape. *** Nurses' school. I approach everything as though I'm going to be slapped in the face. Mom whipped me inconsistently. Never knew where I stood. I learned that a mother gets angry with daughter, and the daughter doesn't want mother to get angry so she allows manipulation.

This is an unexpected example of the development of understanding. While under a slight degree of hypnosis her conscious mind was busy reasoning. She was able to let go of her anxiety and anger.

MALE, LATE 30s NEAR PANIC WHEN
ATTEMPTING TO KISS A WOMAN

*** My dad is trying to get me to learn to use a new tool. Body control and eye movements are hard for me to coordinate. He doesn't understand my nervous problem. *** A gripping. A tightness. I'm at home. In living room. I'm about to kiss this woman. I can't. Anxiety in the pit of my stomach. *** Image of a breast. I bit it!! My mother. It's being taken away from me. I'm abandoned. That explains it. It's OK now.

He verbalized his reasoning and understanding. He later said that dating and kissing his girlfriend were a real pleasure.

FEMALE, LATE 30s
CONFLICTING FEELINGS OVER
FAITH IN GOD

Client had taken religious vows. She had been a novice in a convent. She had dropped out because she had lost faith in God. She was preoccupied with feelings of guilt over her lack of faith.

*** It's spring. Cold. I'm in the house playing. _____ brother] is sick. He had a cold. It's increasingly bad. Worse. My mother is frantic. He's having difficulty breathing. Doctor not available. He's 3. Doctor came. Wrapped him in sheets. Picked him up and carried him out. I'm filled with despair. Daddy went to the hospital. He came back with a priest. Mother is screaming. I knew what death meant. I'll never see him again. I missed him. I felt if God had liked him enough, he wouldn't have done that. I felt we aren't good enough to have better treatment than that. I felt the same way when Daddy died. I still feel that way. I don't trust Him. Suddenly and without warning he pulls the rug out. I just don't trust God.

At the time of taking her vows, the mistrust had been repressed. In the convent and again under authoritarian control, her childhood feelings of parental authority and mistrust in God had been associatively recalled.

She came to understand that God placed us in his system and gave us choices, many of which lead to illness and untimely death. She stated that her faith in God had been restored.

MALE, MID 20s
STUTTERING

*** Just started school. Got hit by big kid. I cried. My father got angry. Then he whipped me. Told me to stop crying. Said if I don't stop crying, he'll whip me harder. Feel like I'm choking. Hard to hold it in.

Client had been unconsciously attempting to hold back sound while attempting to speak. The result was stuttering. After the first session, he was able to speak without defect.

FEMALE. MID 30s
FRUSTRATION, LOW SELF-ESTEEM,
SEXUAL DYSFUNCTION
Following are abstracts from many sessions with this client:

*** Talking with my brother. He wants me to come upstairs. He wants to show me something. I'm 10. In his room. He closes the door. Unzipping his pants. I said I'm leaving. He said he'd tell on me if I did. He wants to put it in my mouth. He said it won't hurt. I don't want to look at him. He says don't tell Mom. I feel angry, dirty, guilty. *** I'm 17. Just read a note from my boss. It said, "I love you. I've always wanted to hold you, kiss you." How could he do that? We've been good friends. I'm a friend to his wife. He won't let me move - no - no!! Please let me go. Trying to kiss me... He let me go.

[Client later said that her marriage had been saved. She had not told me she was contemplating divorce.]

*** I'm 3. Sitting on the car. Want to get down. People. "You're all right where you are. You don't need to get down." Angry. They don't care what I want. *** I want to play, too. Softball with my brothers and all the kids. They won't let me play because I'm stupid and don't know how to play. My mother said so. ** My mom is mad. She spanked me. I went to _____'s house before breakfast. It's unfair. I had to give _____ a note about what we had to do. He had to know about our plans. He was going to come over and we were going to build something.

*** I'm playing in the backyard with my brother and _____. He doesn't think I did it right. Yelling. Walks over to me yelling right in my face. I told him to shut up. He kicked me in the stomach. *** My mother and aunt are in the kitchen. I was just coming in the front door. They didn't hear me. Mom was talking about _____ and _____, how proud she is of them. She said a lot of the time she wished she didn't have to have me around. I thought lately things were better.

*** I'm 14. My mother is angry again. Always angry. Supposed to clean upstairs. She doesn't think I do a good job.

158

She thinks I did it bad on purpose. ** I'm trying to go to sleep. My mother is talking to Dad about me. She can't - she doesn't like me. I'm not the same as _____ and _____. She's so proud of them. If she knew half the things they do, she'd have a fit. *** Those I care about, I can't share. My ideas are not important because I said them. If someone else said them they'd be important.

*** We're in bed. (With whom?) With _____ [her husband]. I just hate it. I don't want to be touched. I don't want to do this at all. The only time I see _____ [husband] pleasant is after we've been in bed together.

*** I can't breathe. It's dark outside. There's a man. Big. He's mean. He came from a riverboat. I was just doing my job. I'm a waitress. In town - a little town by the river. Year is 1802. My name is Ida. He's eating with three other men. They're drinking. Loud. They try to pinch me when I walk by. I don't like it. They're talking about my body. Touching my breasts. ... I'm through at their table. I'm not going back. Time for me to get off work to go home... I'm walking. I hear something. Man followed me. I can't breathe. He pushed me down. He's on top of me. I can't breathe. He's kissing me. He's inside of me. I can't breathe. His friends... Oh - NO!!... I'm walking. Bleeding. I'm in the woods. I died. They left my body.

*** I don't want to have any more children. I'm having a baby... (What is your name?) Name? ... (Are you [client's name]? NO!! ... They're going to take my baby. Going to take him away... I'm home. Made of grass and mud. It's hard. (What color is your skin?) Black. [Client was white.] I love him and he's gone. He never came back. He went on the river. There's crocodiles in the river. They said he died.

*** Tied to the fence. That man tied me. I was getting water. Out here all alone. Name is Sani. I live in the village. He's not of our tribe. He's laughing. I don't know what he'll do. He'll probably kill me. He has his hands on my shoulders. He's rough. Hitting me... He killed me. Cut my throat... I lived in a village. Wooden fence all around. I am still there. Have to go back to my baby. I can't. I have to leave this body. Time to be in another -- next body.

159

She forgave her brother, parents, and the offenders in her "prior lives." She rid herself of sexual dysfunction, became very confident, and succeeded in a new job of wholesale selling.

FEMALE, LATE 20s, OBSESSIVE NEED
FOR ATTENTION, ALWAYS SLEEPY,
COULD NOT KEEP A JOB
(recently fired from a responsible job)

*** Seated at my desk. Something is preventing me from cleaning up the area. Sinking feeling like I don't have the ability. I'm not part of it. I pretend it isn't important. *** Mom is yelling at me when I try to clean up my room. *** Dad is yelling at me for taking money for doughnuts. *** Ashamed. In college. Everyone is gathered in my room to look at the big mess in my closet. [She was getting the attention she needed.] *** In nursery at hospital. Lonely. They don't pay attention to me any more. New babies get the attention. I see a lady in white leaning against the wall. She's not doing anything. I cry to get her to come and pick me up but she ignores me.

*** Mom told me I was pudgy. That's ugly. I ate so I wouldn't go to sleep. *** In kindergarten. Teacher wrote on my report card that I thought I was the only child in the world. Needed too much attention. *** In the crib. Smoldering with anger. Bedroom door closed. Baby spoon in my right hand. I am not supposed to cry. All I'm supposed to do is eat, sleep, and mess my diaper. *** Little apartment. First born [newly born]. Mom said, "I want you to go to sleep." Alert all the time. My mother kept saying, "Go to sleep." When I go to sleep is the only time she said I was a good girl. Also she doesn't go away while I'm eating [breast feeding]. I eat so she won't go away.

*** In a bunk bed in the dining room. We had a fire. They're painting. Mom is saying I have to stay in bed. In crib - patting me on the bottom. She'll like me better if I go to sleep. *** I'm at work. Have child's feelings. Sleepy. Someone has arm around me. A slender lady. Not lonely. Someone to be with. *** In my crib. Lonely. Don't want my parents to leave me alone anymore. Alone in the bedroom. Mom talks to me as long as I eat so I keep

160

eating so she'll talk to me. I go to sleep cause there's nothing else to do.

*** In the hospital. I'm getting bigger and madder. Everybody was real excited when I was born. Then "plunk" - nothing. *** In crib. I'm turning in on myself. I want to go back - not be aware anymore. *** My brother was born. I wanted to be a boy so Daddy would love me. He's in a crib. My daddy says, "I've always wanted a boy." *** Floating. Warm. I'm not born yet. Someone is shouting. My mother is saying, "I don't want this G__ D___ baby." *** At work. Crying. Lonely. Very sad. I'd rather feel sad over loneliness than to feel sad that someone doesn't like you. *** Feel wiped out. Mommy yells at me. Wants me to go outside. The peace can't last. She's throwing me away. I'm supposed to be dead when I'm out there. No life to me out there.

*** I want to stay where she's cooing over the new baby but I want her to like me too. *** I'm in the living room. I'm 3. Sitting over against the wall alone. Mommy and Daddy and Grandma and Grandpa are across the room with the new baby. Just came home from the hospital. I can't see my hands. (What are you wearing?) I can't see my body. (What color are your shoes?) I can't see my feet. I'm invisible. I must be because I keep waving at them over there and they don't pay any attention to me so they must not see me. I must be invisible.

*** I'm at the office. Can't seem to pick up the phone. I have to make calls to make more sales. Want to beat my quota but am not even making it. *** I'm in 4th grade. My teacher won't let me answer more than so many questions. If I answer right more than three times I'm wrong so I fuzzy my thinking and when I grow up I can't even talk to people. *** At work. I'm afraid others will go away if I keep selling. *** My sister. I was always outsmarting her and she dropped out of the competition. I shouldn't have. As long as I have competition I'm not alone.

*** I have a new job. A few weeks ago. I'm home. Cleaning under the sink. (What day is it?) Friday. (What time is it?) 8 o'clock. (Don't you work on Fridays?) Yes, but I have to clean under the sink. (Won't you be late for work?) Yes, but I have to clean under the sink. When I get to work, Mr. [name] will call me into his office. *** I'm at work. Came in late. He fired me but at least he talked to me. [Coming in late was one of her ways of getting attention.]

After an inordinate number of sessions the client was able to function on the job and her social relations improved significantly. However she admitted she was still seeking attention. [Contrary to advice, client terminated. Further treatment was indicated.]

FEMALE, LATE 20s
FEAR, STRESS, FEELING REJECTED

*** I have a feeling that Mom's lurking in the background. I remember being afraid of getting stabbed. Always waiting for Mom to blow up. I'm afraid people are going to be like Mom and Dad and blow up at me. *** Dad yelled at me on the intercom. Tells me to shut up and go to sleep. I was hoping to hear something nice. *** Hurts because you won't hug me. [While in the hypnotic state, she had asked the author to hug her.] (Find that feeling another time, another place.) I'm a little kid. A baby. I'm reaching out for Mom. She shoved me away, back into the crib. It hurts so much.

*** I want to be perfect. I'm 7. At the same time I hope that I might end up having my head covered with sh__, permanently. Then Mom and Dad wouldn't recognize me. But I'd be more completely alone then than I was. Hurts so deeply when people don't see who you are. *** Mom's drinking. Drunk. Dripping all over us. She had never loved us all these years. I couldn't stand to be touched by her. *** I'm 6 months old. Mom carrying me. She's very angry. Scared me. She's walking fast. Dropped me in the crib.

*** Mom's drunk. Following me upstairs. I feel guilty. She and Dad separated. I don't want to touch her at all. I feel used, disgusted, guilty. *** Pain in jaws. I'm 8. I feel so alone. I'm biting down. *** I'm in Mom and Dad's bed with baby sitter's boy friend and my sister. He's playing with us. I like the attention, the affection. He took his clothes off. Tickling my genitals. I'm scared but it feels good. He says I'm supposed to do

162

the same thing to him. I have to do what he says. His penis is so big. I feel like I'm going to suffocate. In my mouth. He's rough. Mean. Holding me. I feel like biting. He threatened to hurt me if I tell. After, he doesn't want anything to do with us.

*** I'm inside Mom. In her womb. She's really angry. She hit me through her belly. She's yelling, "Get out!" I heard her crying later.

*** Big feast. Bagpipes. Scotland. [She later said she had never been there.] Everybody's there from the whole area. It's after dinner. My father and others are playing bagpipes. The rest of us are watching. I'm playing in the barn. Grandfather. He puts me on his penis. I'm afraid - the next time - and the next time - and the next time. *** I'm 7. Wanted a toy car for Christmas. Badly. But I know I can't say anything about my grandfather.

Client's symptoms disappeared and she terminated against my advice. Because the early associated memories were being recalled so rapidly just before termination, I concluded that there were more underlying negative experiences.

MALE, MID 40s ANXIETY, SEXUAL DYSFUNCTION, COMPULSIVE BEHAVIOR

[This is an exceptionally long but very educational abstract. It provides added insight and may significantly contribute to one's ability to forgive.]

Regardless of the weather, client went outside for a walk alone every night. He felt compelled to find a lighted bedroom window where he could watch the couple engaged in sexual activity including intercourse. He knew all the likely locations for many blocks around his home. He had experienced the compulsion since age 16. Client had erroneously presented the problem as voyeurism, one of the features of which is sexual pleasure. He had not experienced sexual pleasure during his nightly sojourns.

Client could not control his behavior. He fully realized that he risked imprisonment, the loss of his family, being ostracized by many, and because of the nature of his job, he assuredly would have been fired immediately.]

*** Pressure at school. Feel stupid for not answering questions. *** Feel fear. In tap dancing class. Costs a lot of money. My folks are not rich. *** I want the same things my older brother is getting. He's going to school with a new sweater. *** Watching a couple through a window. I'm wondering what it is that they feel toward each other. What it is they have that I don't have? The anxiety comes before. Watching them is almost a blank period. Afterward I feel guilty, fear, feel I wasted my time. I get angry. I want to blame other people so I don't feel guilty. Want to change but not able to change. Disappointed. Here I go again. Before, it's anxiety. I know I shouldn't. Quick tug-of-war. And then I go and do it again.

*** I feel curiosity. Wanting to see my mother naked. To see what she looks like. *** Having fun with my friends. Teacher is standing. She's angry. Positioning of her head is important. Not on my level. Looking down. Angry. All of a sudden I learned it's wrong to have such a good feeling. *** My mother. In bed. Her back is to me. Want to see and feel her abdomen and her breasts. Almost like a child wanting to be touched. Her genital area all dark. What's there? I'm curious. If I touch her or look, I'll be denied the other, the comfort of her. *** I'm smaller. Sliding off her stomach. Almost underneath. Something separating us. I know she's there, but we're separate. I'll never be inside her again. We were together, but never again. But I would feel loved if I were back inside!!

*** With my wife. Her back is to me. I can't express to her back. It's the position. I need to face her. It's more than just sex. It's someone turning their back to me. Not acknowledging. Not responding. Almost like I'm forcing rather than giving. Giving is important. *** I feel like I'm stretched out on the floor. Like I'm stretched over something. Like a rod down my back. Pain. My mother. Tension. I'm sliding. But the pressure is behind. The black hole is receding. I see my mother's legs. I'm out. I'm free. Curious. Shiny metal. Lights. Mother. I see her thigh. [A newborns sight is blurred.] Her crotch. I see a black hole. Small. *I want to see*. Almost as though I can crawl back inside. I want to crawl back in. I'm cold. And small. Curious and wanting to know. I want to see where I came from. And that's what's

164

endangering me....... [He had become aware of part of the reason for his willingness to run the risk of prison.] I can be curious about what I want to be curious.

*** I'm inside. Warm. Comfortable. Two people running their hands over stomach. Male voice is soft. Female voice is loving. They sound happy. Don't know if I'm a boy or girl. Feel conflict. *** I'm outside. It's cold. I want to be back inside. *I want to look* and I want to be inside. I don't want to be lonely. I want to be loved. *** I'm in a grove of trees. I'm sitting on a rock. Rays of sunlight on me. Warm. It's damp. My head in my hands. I've been abandoned and I'm all alone. I'm a strong person. A respected person. All of a sudden I'm alone. They've all left. I'm afraid of the unknown. I'm a leader. All of my followers have gone. Horses. Tents. Food. They wanted to go back where it's safe. I wanted to take the risk.... It's painful, but I'm OK.

*** (Are you aware what will happen if you are caught looking in the windows?) I'll look just one more time. *** I'll take just one more cookie. No one will ever know. And I do it over and over. And pretty soon all the cookies are gone. [He had developed a childhood belief that he would not get caught.] *** I don't want to let go of something that is good. I want to be inside where it's warm. Back inside Mom. [Client started crying.] I can't go back. Not ever. I can't go back inside. I can't undisappoint myself. *** If I can get away with it, it's OK. If I can write, "I will not talk in class" 25 times without my mother finding out, it's OK.

*** I'm in school. Nap time. Rugs. I've been bad. Teacher made me put my rug in front of her desk. I look under her desk. Look up her dress. Focused on it. I pulled away. Didn't think I should do that, but I looked again, and again, and again. *** I'm back to wanting to be inside my mother. *** I stole a candy bar. Didn't get caught. I took some baking chocolate and hid it. My secret. Nobody caught me. Feeling of being smart because I got away with it.

*** (Imagine you are standing on the sidewalk with your dogs. You see a lighted bedroom window. You know you should not look in but you are feeling something in conflict.) It has to do with love, with my mother, being naked, feeling lonely, rejected. I want to be loved. Don't want to be lonely. I can find love by climbing back inside. Or, by going and *looking*! *** I want my mother and don't want her. I want to be back inside and I want to be free.

It was his desire to look, to see where he had come from, that caused the compulsion to view a woman's vagina, but not because of any sexual pleasure. He had been seeking the peaceful feeling that he had in his mother's womb. Client had repeatedly not been caught during childhood misbehavior. He had developed a *childhood* belief that he would not get caught. This contributed to his *adult* belief that he would not be caught. He resolved the compulsion, anxiety, and sexual dysfunction. He called several months later and said he and his wife had fallen in love all over again.

Precautions Regarding Hypnosis

Hypnotists commonly claim that a person will never do anything under hypnosis that the person would not otherwise do. WRONG! Based on my own experiences and reading of others' experiences, I have concluded that a subject in a state of hypnosis will respond to a suggestion only if the suggestion is acceptable to the subject's unconscious, i.e., if there is not a stronger unconscious belief in conflict with the suggestion. *However*, suppose a male hypnotist suggests to a female client that she is with her husband. The suggestion is likely acceptable to the subject. She loves her husband. In her mind, the hypnotist has now become her husband. The next suggestion is that she and her husband go to bed. Also acceptable. And then what? If the therapist is not a moral person, her experience can be devastating.

A hypnotist could suggest to a subject that he feels warm and this is a good day for a swim, acceptable suggestions. He suggests that the pool is on the roof of the office building. Acceptable. The two go to the roof. A suggestion is made that the subject is wearing swim trunks. Acceptable. Looking down, he sees his chest, swimming trunks, and bare feet. While standing *at the edge of the roof*, the next suggestion is to look at the beautiful pool. Acceptable (The fantasized pool and surrounding deck start near the edge of the roof and project out over the street.) A very final acceptable suggestion could be to dive into the pool. Acceptable.

Not all hypnotists are aware of what can happen during hypnosis sessions. Some are unaware that a subject in the hypnotic state, without even a suggestion, may choose to regress to earlier traumatic experiences. The subject may require knowledgeable explanations and support to get through the anger, depression, rage, grief, fear, terror, hopelessness, or worse.

Hypnotic suggestion that serious or severe pain be ignored or subdued may cause symptoms to completely disappear. **This should be considered only as first aid**. Especially if the pain is internal, a physician should be contacted *immediately*. What if an appendix or colon were on the verge of rupturing, or already has? You may wish to make your family and friends aware of these precautions.

If you decide to undergo hypnotherapy, choose carefully. Many "quacks" have purchased degrees from diploma mills. A large number of qualified healthcare professionals are experienced in hypnotherapy but may very likely use different approaches. Ask if the professional you tentatively select is willing to meet with you for a brief no-fee session. This will give you an opportunity to question about training, qualifications, and experience. Ask him to briefly relate a few therapy session abstracts. He can do this without identifying those involved.

Chapter 11
CRIME AND CONSEQUENCES

One Consequence - Stress

Crime stresses all of society. We are stressed if defrauded. We are stressed from fear of street gangs and paroled repeat sex offenders and violent criminals. Women, and even men in prison, are stressed by fear of rape and brutality. We are stressed by the loss of a loved one killed by a murderous drunken driver. We are stressed by violence. We remain stressed for a long time if we are robbed or if our homes are burglarized. We are stressed by financial loss through white collar crime. We are even stressed by the thought of or behavior of others who are stressed. We may feel their pain. Steps can be taken to reduce crime and its stressful effects. Congress, schools, parents, teachers, you, and I each have a role. Now is not soon enough. Action by voters is long overdue.

Society has chosen to imprison most convicted criminals. The objective is to remove them from society. It has been hoped that doing so would deter them and other potential criminals. The system has not worked. One large prison recently reported 92% recidivism. The high rate of return shouts that we need a better approach to discipline and rehabilitation. This nation is long overdue in taking steps to cause criminals to believe the consequences of criminal acts. It is for their long range good as well as for ours.

Easy unproductive prison life, too many amenities, early paroles, loopholes in the law, liberal courts, and previous overly-permissive Supreme Court justices that too often have legislated rather than interpret the constitution, have all contributed to the problem, even fostered it. There are some who have a phobia of offending the offenders.

A belief that punishment should fit the crime does not preclude understanding, forgiveness, and love for criminals. For the past six years I have spent one afternoon each week in a state prison helping inmates to resolve their feelings of anger, rage, low self-esteem, and even more complex emotions regarding those who severely abused them during childhood.

I do not believe in capital punishment for two reasons. First, I do not believe we have a right to take a person's life. Second, I know how mistaken people can be because of biases and misperceptions. Approximately eighty inmates condemned to death have since been found innocent through DNA tests and other irrefutable evidence.

White Collar Blue Collar

White collar criminals may have done more damage to, and killed more people, albeit slowly, than all of the armed and violent criminals combined. Financial losses can be devastating. Stress kills slowly but surely. Emotionally caused illness causes a slow but too-early death just as certain as if killed by a gun. Legislators and the justice system have distinguished between "high-class felons" "and "low-class felons", between "fast murderers" and "slow murderers." Slowly killing hundreds of people by stealing millions of dollars through fraud is a classier crime than stealing a few hundred dollars from a convenience food store, or than quickly shooting and killing the clerk.

The classier criminal somehow rates a classier prison and for a much shorter period of time. This week a news article told of a man who had been found guilty of embezzling $800,000. His sentence was retroactive and limited to time served. He had been in jail eleven months waiting for trial. An inmate in State prison had stolen a six-pack of beer. This is a felony if one is already a felon. Because of the three strikes law, he was sentenced to life in prison. Fear of lengthy incarceration in hard-time prisons would be a deterrent to white-collar greed, but they do not fear it because it seemingly never happens. Their terms are shorter and in relatively pleasant facilities.

Believed Consequences, a Deterrent

Many criminals have not been given enough reason to regret inappropriate and violent behavior in the home, school, or neighborhood. During childhood they were not taught and trained to believe that moral behavior was, is, and will be important. They had not been convinced of, and did not believe that punitive consequences would affect them if they were to turn to crime. Many were abused, some viciously and repeatedly. Anger accumulated to the point of being explosive, and it *did* explode. Many were criticized, ridiculed, or abandoned by one or both parents. Self-esteem is under the rug. Material things are needed in an attempt to build self-esteem. The money to buy them is obtained through fraud, burglary, or robberies often resulting in violence and gunfire.

Criminals and potential criminals would benefit if they were to believe *the punishment will fit the crime*. Parents must be convinced to not anger their children, to treat them with respect, and to teach, train, and convince them of the consequences of crime.

Convicted criminals must be caused to regret their crimes, *to believe the consequences of repeating*. The regret and belief must be strong enough so that they convince youths, parents, and all others. Punishment must be *fair*. Sentences must be determined and implemented irrespective of reputation, wealth, friendships, politics, race, creed, color, sex, age, white or blue collar, or any other personal community or business standing. Criminals will be inhibited from committing crime only by fearful *beliefs* of the consequences to themselves, or by strengthening moral beliefs.

Right now, parents should start building the beliefs in the minds of their children. School classroom viewing of videos and graphics would emphasize the consequences of crime. Prisons could *teach* inmates the consequences of repeat offenses until they develop unconscious beliefs, not just conscious understanding. If a potential criminal's behavior is to be desirably controlled it will be *only through moral beliefs, moral consciences, and unconscious beliefs regarding consequences of criminal behavior*.

Compare

This is not commiserating. It is only a statement of facts for comparison. In the WW2 U.S. Navy, during boot camp we slept in hammocks, 60 to a compartment. Enlisted personnel on smaller vessels (I can speak for destroyers) had no amenities. Our sleeping accommodations were *end to end* bunks three and four deep. Except for what we wore or carried with us, each individual's belongings were kept in three-cubic-foot lockers or in a sea-bag. Toilets consisted of rows of seats, elbow to elbow, on long slanted metal tanks with water flowing from one end, down the length of the tank to the drain at the other end.

Commissioned officers had free and easy access to any enlisted areas at any time. There was zero privacy. We had no dentist or medical doctor within many hundreds of miles. We went to sea with one 3rd class cook aboard. I was told we should have had one 1st class, one $2^{nd\ class}$, and two 3rd class cooks. Need I tell you about the food? We were in hot climates with no refrigerated air conditioning. We were in the north Atlantic during winter with many having no foul weather clothing. *And we had it good* compared to most of the millions in ground combat and the Pacific Fleet.

There were no do-gooder civil liberties or civil rights groups who expressed care or concern, and I did not expect them to do so. There was reason for all of the above. We were at war. *We still are*, but of a different kind. It is time to resolve to win and to act on that resolution.

Four Walls Need Not a Prison Make

Let hi-tech do the confinement at a much lower cost. Organized loud and articulate do-gooders fight for better care of the uncaring. As a result, we build prisons at costs up to $100,000+ per inmate. That is several years of nationwide average per capita income. We also spend considerably more than a typical annual income to maintain each prisoner, as much as $60,000 per year in New York. These costs will inflate. This week I read of several planned federal prisons with large

172

swimming pools and *meditation pools*!?!

The classier prisons provide movies, television, radios, libraries, recreation areas, and expensively equipped exercise rooms envied by the working taxpayer. Inmates are provided good food, medical and dental care, and cells which are roomier per person than navy shipboard quarters. Some prisons have removed some of the amenities because of public outcry.

Incorrigible criminals can be kept from society permanently. We need not spend as much money doing the job as in the past. We can provide quarters equivalent to navy quarters as described. We can put inmates to work to pay much of the costs.

We need not provide a country club atmosphere for any prisoner, including the classy white-collar felons. Why do we provide better facilities for those who are destroying our nation than to those who worked at saving it? Why are we concerned more about the rights of criminals than about the rights of victims? We are all victims in one way or another. Stress kills. Why are we more concerned in caring for the uncaring than in caring for those who care? *I am not suggesting that we not care about prisoners.* I *am* suggesting that we *attempt to cut crime and costs.*

Low-budget prisons can be built. Build the types of barracks that millions of wartime military have used, or use facilities at closed military bases. They can be adapted. Containment of inmates within the prison grounds need not be complicated or expensive. Continue to surround the prison complexes with high chain link fences with razor wire at the top. Within, and parallel to them, build electric fences. Within those, build low rail fences or walls only to serve as warnings. Photo electric cells or laser systems can give instant warning of anyone's coming within a few feet of the rail fences. Capacitance proximity alarms can detect anyone near the photo-electric cells or approaching any of the security devices. I built a proximity alarm in 1938. Tamper proof proximity detectors can be easily designed and built. Provide backup electrical generating systems.

Security is more than keeping inmates incarcerated. It includes keeping them safe from each other. It includes detecting abusive substances. Use dogs for drug detection. Spot-check every day. Stop violence and sexual abuse within the prisons. Set up video surveillance capable of spot-check monitoring of every square foot inside all buildings and in the yards. Maintain after-dark low level of lighting to allow 24 hour per day randomly selected area surveillance. Why not? Shipboard compartments were always lighted. I remind you of experiencing a total lack of privacy in the military. This may require reassignment of guards based on gender. I believe this has always been proper. Male inmates have told me they deeply resent women guards' walking into their shower rooms. I would expect to find that most women strenuously object to male guards.

A recently former governor of California mentioned that the state had issued temporary work and entry permits to several hundred thousand foreigners because of the work needed to be done in the state. I know a citizen, an inmate at that time, who along with many other inmates, had spent years watching TV, exercising with expensive equipment, and reading in the prison library. Isn't there something wrong here?

Many authorities and lawmakers suggest training inmates in vocations to enable them to earn a living after release. Those authorities must believe that work will be available, and that there is a need for labor. *If we believe that*, and if it *is true*, bring the work into the prisons. Private industry will feel threatened by this. They can compete with the prison industries or bid on and profit from managing them. Inmates can be productive while learning. Many are already skilled. Nearly every inmate I encounter wants to work. Yesterday, interest rates were raised to deter inflation that otherwise might result because of a current nationwide labor shortage.

Work in prisons can be allocated even to the most dangerous and violent inmates. Many work tasks could be performed by incorrigibles even in isolation. No work, no eat. Why not? *We* work to eat.

Work can also be performed outside the prison by inmates. I am not suggesting we return to Georgia chain gangs. Closely monitoring them is no problem with existing technology. They could work in what could be called BGs, braceleted groups. Leaving the work area by only a very few feet would trigger an

174

alarm. All bracelets within a BG can be continually and automatically electronically queried every second. They can also transmit from one to another in a figurative ring. Failure to respond would instantly trigger an alarm. I.e., If one wanders even slightly, an alarm is triggered. If an alarm bracelet is cut, covered with a shield, or deactivated, continuous *automatic interactivity* among the BG's ring of bracelets would be instantly broken. An alarm would be triggered immediately. Easy. The costs are miniscule compared to the benefits. BGs could be quartered in proximity and the same system would assure security at night. Bracelets could be switched on/off or from one BG to another by radio control.

Inmates could be assigned to a myriad of types of work. They could manufacture products. They could repair roads and highways, rebuild our dangerously deteriorated bridges, and repair publicly owned buildings. Much is in need of repair. Among prisoners can be found very intelligent skilled and unskilled workers, apprentices, accountants, supervisors, and managers, whatever is needed in men's or women's facilities.

Require that all inmates who work be paid the same as law abiding citizens who do equivalent work. You and I pay for *our* costs of living. Importantly require that they pay for all of the identifiable costs of their crimes including incarceration, food, and shelter. Withhold income taxes, Social Security taxes, court costs, fees for medical and dental care, and major medical insurance. Withhold the cost of room, board, clothing, laundering, shoes, required haircuts, movies, TV, use of exercise equipment, prison administration, and payments to persons and organizations that were victimized.

I cannot think of a reason why their personal resources should not be confiscated including a portion of future earnings, until the debt to victims and society has been paid in full. Freeze and confiscate all resources retroactively to the date of crime to prevent sheltering through gifts, foreign bank deposits, single premium insurance policies, or other devious attempts to avoid payment. Make all of this a part of sentencing. Why should victims suffer a lifetime while the offenders do not? And why should taxpayers pay? Why is this tolerated?

Elderly longtime inmates will have earned a Social Security retirement. They can be required to continue paying at least a part of the expense. Each inmate, including those drawing social security, can be left with only enough money for personal expenses. Cruel? Consider the poor elderly person on Social Security and Medicaid, in a nursing home, and left with only a very small amount of money, currently $30, for personal effects. Whom should we treat better?

Inmates, and especially lifers, may manifest an attitude of unwillingness to work at an appropriate rate or not at all. If they balk at work, withhold every amenity and put them on a substantive but extremely austere diet. If they do not respond, isolate them during non-working hours. Another approach would be in-cell piecework with food issued in return for completed work. Fasting would be rare. Again, *no work no eat.*

Inmates can be given the opportunity to receive higher levels of education and earn scholastic degrees by going to in-prison classes during non-working hours. Thousands of others and I went to night school and paid for it. If they are paid for their work, they too can pay for the tuition. If they do not earn enough in prison, they can pay later as do those outside who have student loans. Scholarships can be awarded for outstanding performance.

The administration of all of this would be complex but justified. Costs to the taxpayer would be reduced. Inmate self-esteem would rise. Interaction during working hours would socialize many of the antisocial. Training and experience would be a giant leap in rehabilitation.

Invalid Excuses

Many activists and some politicians decry the prosecution of young criminals. What are they contributing to the reduction of juvenile crime? They blame the crime rate on the lack of education and availability of jobs, and on low income.

If the young are willing to work, jobs are available, albeit menial work. I have shined shoes, mowed lawns, pitched hay, dug post holes, pulled mustard weed out of wheat fields, washed and waxed cars, worked as a bus boy, and cleaned up dog dung seven days a week. Education was not a consideration. Low income was not a consideration. Eating, clothing, and shelter were. Too many young persons simply feel and believe they are above such jobs. Many believe that a menial job is not a step to a better job, so why try? That does not license them to commit crimes. Many of our young have the unconscious belief that crime and violence are OK, or they do not unconsciously believe that they will be severely punished if caught and convicted. *That can be changed*.

Prevention Begins at Home

Crime in the schools must be perceived and punished for the crime that it is. Violent criminals of any age must be removed from society. Formerly, children who committed crimes were not yet viewed as habitual or dangerous criminals. In too many cases they were and still are being let off with minor disciplinary action.

Many young children are already the ultimate criminal. It is common knowledge that some carry lethal weapons to school. They terrorize other children, teachers, neighbors and even their own parents. They kill. Too often their parents have not accepted responsibility for teaching and training. Neither school systems nor the justice systems have the resources to mitigate behavioral and emotional problems in the young. If the overall picture does not change, society's stress will continue its uptrend.

School, school bus, schoolyard, and street behavior of the young violent criminal must change, or he must be removed from the school system and from society. If violent young criminals are not tried in court as adults, we can expect a continuation of the trend toward more violence. If they *are* tried, convicted, and incarcerated, other young people will begin to believe the consequences of crime. However, we need special work/school facilities for incarceration of children who are tried as adults and convicted. They simply *must not* be thrown in with adult inmates. Nor should they be placed with non-violent young criminals. High school classes are essential.

Everyone has a need to feel secure. Many in society are being slowly killed by the stress from not feeling secure. Even children stress children. If a minor student carries a gun or any other weapon to school, why not hold the parents responsible? If parents receive legal disciplinary action, more of them will care enough to teach, train, and monitor their children starting when they are very young.

If parents were to know *and believe* that criminals, irrespective of age, were to be held accountable, they would do more to teach and train their children. Belief that a son's or daughter's involvement in crime will result in conviction and incarceration is a strong motivator for parents to build a child's conscience, to strengthen his belief of the consequences of crime. Most parents want their children to lead moral lives. Parents want their children to avoid punishment. One would expect them to do something about it, but it is clear that many do not. Children properly taught and trained will develop the belief that crime really does not pay, that it violates the laws of God and man, and that it *will bring punishment.*

Children can be trained to lead reasonably disciplined lives. Permissiveness will not get the desired results, not with children, not with potential criminals, and not with inmates.

We, the Voters

We are becoming a better-educated nation, but in what? Many criminals, white collar and otherwise, are brilliantly intelligent and street-smart. Writers of crime stories for TV, computer games, movies, and books are contributing their genius to the teaching of criminality and violence. Many welfare recipients have become experts at defrauding the system. They are unconvicted felons. They teach each other and their children. Instead of working at solving the problem, many legislators turn blind and deaf to the problems. "I need their votes."

One mother was collecting government money for each of her four children. Somehow she had convinced authorities that all were mentally ill even though attending and seriously misbehaving in public school. A TV interviewer asked one of the

178

children why she was acting the way she did in school. Her answer was, "My mother says that if we don't act that way, we won't get our crazy-money." For each of four children, the mother received several hundred dollars per month. The mother was teaching her children to be felons and causing them to commit felonies. We, the taxpayers tolerate it. Worse, we vote for those who facilitate the process.

This may also give you pause. During a brief encounter an inmate told me that he had been receiving $1200 per month from the Social Security Administration. I asked why. He said, "Because I have been in trouble with drugs nearly all my life." He said it had been cut to $900 several years ago but he had gotten it restored.

"Who's watching the store?" The President and Congress assuredly are not. But whose fault is that. Who voted years ago and elected the President that appointed the liberal and permissive Supreme Court judges that, at the time, set the tone for the entire Justice System for decades? Is this what you want? Too many otherwise usually moral persons do not see voting as a moral issue. Failure to vote for moral legislators and other government officials, including the President, perpetuates immorality.

None of this chapter was written because of lack of love for humanity. It is the reverse. Tough love is always appropriate. We understand that convicts are emotionally driven and inhibited. The result was, is, and will be criminal behavior until unconscious beliefs are changed. However, even though we understand, we need not, should not, and must not tolerate a person's actions that reduce the quality and length of our lives. We can love without condoning or tolerating criminal behavior. The do-gooders could do more good by turning their efforts toward promoting good for society, rather than for those who are destroying it.

I care about and respect the inmates but abhor much of their behavior that put them in prison. Among the crimes they have committed are multiple murders, rape, brutal beatings, violent robberies, and some I shall not mention. With Holy Scripture I attempt to validate my beliefs regarding unconscious emotionally driven and emotionally inhibited behavior. It works. No prisoner in attendance has ever objected to my referencing the Bible. It is loaded with wisdom. Inmates often refer to the proof before I do. It is my fervent hope that I can continue working with them.

Chapter 12
ONCE MORE FOR THE ROAD

What? Again?

As you know, no human on Earth can ever be perfect. No one can achieve a tolerance level of 100%. Christianity's eleventh commandment (John 13:34) tells us to love one another, no conditions. We simply cannot love everyone, but we *can work toward* being able to love and tolerate more people. What a beautiful world this could be if everyone would just make an effort. Sadly, it is not happening and never will.

If you already know, and understand and believe what you are going to read in the next five minutes, hooray! You will easily forgive, and can tolerate and will benefit from the repetition. It builds and strengthens beliefs. I would be delighted if I could know that you will breeze through this chapter thinking, "I already know that. I have read that before. I understood that the first time, and the second, and.... I know that, too. Of course. That's obvious. Same-o same-o. Here we go again."

The author's objective was and is to bring the reader to an unconsciously believed understanding of self and others, to the ability to forgive, to accept circumstance, and to feel better.

Negativity causes stress. Stress kills. The body is stressed by associative recall of previously formed negative desires, beliefs, and emotions. Sensing aspects of today's environment serves as reminders of past experiences when similar environmental aspects were sensed. Stress may be felt without any awareness of its effect on the body. Emotions may be recalled and felt without awareness as to why. Whether positive or negative, they drive and inhibit behavior.

As much as one likes to think and believe that he is in conscious control of his behavior, abstracts of therapy sessions have provided evidence that behavior is emotionally driven and inhibited, and is not consciously controlled. If a conscious decision is implemented, it is because at the time of the decision and in that environment, the unconscious belief system is in agreement and is not manifesting a belief in conflict with the *conscious* belief. This is why it is so critically important to develop a moral belief system, a moral conscience, and to continue strengthening positive and moral beliefs.

Since infancy and even while in the mother's womb, memories of significant experiences have been stored in long term memory in the unconscious. Experiences include physical feelings, unfulfilled desires, conclusions, emotions felt during each experience, and whatever is perceptually sensed in the environment with any of the five senses. All are associatively linked in memory. Recall of one may recall any or all of the others. Whatever is currently sensed in the environment serves as a reminder of earlier experiences. Unconscious beliefs are associatively recalled. Emotions are felt. Unfulfilled desires rise. Some may healthily motivate us to succeed or exceed in moral efforts. Others may drive us to negative behavior. Still others may inhibit us from even attempting what we logically know to be good for us.

At times, associatively recalled beliefs may be in conflict with moral, logical, and conscious beliefs. Recalled emotions may range from feelings of happiness and confidence to those of helplessness and depression. Conflicting emotions and beliefs may rise simultaneously as if multiplexed. They cause action, reaction, overreaction, inhibition, or outright prevention. "I want to and don't want to." "I love him, but I hate him." "I know it's wrong to smoke and I want to quit but I can't." The unconscious affects interpersonal relationships in school, at home, in the workplace, and in social life.

Early repetitive treatment predisposes a child to expect similar treatment in the future and at times to misperceive the actions and intents of others. Negativity starts when a child is offended or when he misperceives loving care in the form of parental control as offensive. He believes that adults do not listen and do not care enough to explain. He is too often not satisfied with the outcome. Positive experiences build confidence and self-esteem. These experiences are the foundation of adult desires, beliefs, and emotions.

If a child misbehaves, his parent may feel a childlike desire of wanting to hit back or a need to feel superior. He may be too preoccupied to devote time to a child. He is emotionally driven and inhibited. He may be ignorant of a child's needs. He offends his child. If this type of treatment is repetitious, the child develops low self-esteem and feelings of wanting revenge and of unfairness and anger, even at God. He misbehaves. The sins of the fathers are taking effect.

Within the family system, each member's behavior affects every other member now and into the future. Each family member is a part of every other member's environment. Each child develops a different set of desires, beliefs, and emotions, and in different degrees. With parental understanding and parenting skills, the development of negativity can be significantly reduced. A child can be guided toward the development of positive desires, beliefs, and emotions. Solomon told us to train the children. Training must be moral, caring, and sustained. Parenting includes teaching and training, reasonable control, disciplinary action, giving *appropriate* latitude, and demonstrated love and respect. Children deserve to be happy and to feel safe and secure. Adults must accept that responsibility.

Violence or incest devastates a family. A battered wife may remain in her situation out of feelings of fear, feelings of dependency, and a need to be loved. A battered child has such a powerful need for love that, out of fear of losing or never receiving that love, he likely will not tell anyone of the abuse. Love and forgiveness do not imply approval or tolerance, nor do they preclude moral responsibilities of the observer or victim. Whoever becomes aware of abuse of any kind must morally report it promptly. Anyone can be a victim of physical abuse. Abuse in the home continues until someone "blows the whistle." If unreported, the abuser has no reason to stop. He believes he can get away with abuse in the family. A sexual abuser of children may range far and wide and for a lifetime, or until he is reported or caught in the act.

Courts do not understand a physically, emotionally, or sexually abused child and the depth of his fear and emotional pain. Facing the abuser, the child, previously threatened even with death, may be too fearful to disclose the truth in front of the abuser. Courts are in need of change.

Forgiveness is essential to acquiring and maintaining physical, emotional, and spiritual health. Merely speaking words of forgiveness is not enough. Forgiveness is genuine only through unconsciously believed understanding of the whys of emotionally driven and emotionally inhibited behavior of offenders. Behavioral drives and inhibitions trace back to childhood when others were in control. It is not our fault that we have negative desires, beliefs, and emotional needs that drive and inhibit our behavior. The same is true of those who may have offended us. If we understand that, and unconsciously believe what it is that we understand, we can forgive anyone for anything.

Memories of anger, resentment, rejection, and desires for revenge are stored in the unconscious. The forgiver will know that his forgiveness is real when offenses can be remembered without recalling and refeeling the associated negative emotions. With unconsciously believed understanding, forgiveness occurs automatically. It can be felt even while being subjected to offensive behavior. Negative emotions may then reduce to the point of often being unidentifiable and not felt.

Circumstance is another source of negativity and stress. It often causes feelings of unfairness, helplessness, even hopelessness. It may be imposed on a child by significant others. Every young child is trapped in his world of circumstance. It may also be imposed by random encounters with non-significant others, or by random so-called acts-of-God. Adults are in charge and may mistreat the young who cannot understand the whys. During adulthood, reduction of stress and negative emotions results from acceptance of negative circumstance without the thoughts of "Poor me," "Why me?" or "Why is God doing this to me?" "Why does God let this happen?" Essential to health is the acceptance of the randomness and uncontrollability of circumstance and getting on with living and *doing*.

Resolution of stress in the workplace reduces stress of loved ones and others. Understanding problems in the workplace will assist in deciding whether to leave or stay, and in selecting a low-stress job or workplace. With understanding and forgiveness, feelings of envy, fear, resentment, and anger toward superiors, subordinates, and peers will reduce or even disappear. Feelings of frustration, helplessness, and of feeling trapped in a job will lessen. Driving to and from work will be less stressful.

We are creatures of inner conflict. We may feel up one day and down the next. Negative sides of the inner conflicts are reduced or overwhelmed by acceptance of circumstance, and by developing an unconsciously believed understanding of emotionally driven and emotionally inhibited behavior. Forgiveness of offenders is then automatic. Stress and anxiety are reduced. Emotional, physical, and spiritual health improve. Barring circumstance, we live longer and feel better while doing so.

All of society has a responsibility to make believers out of criminals and potential criminals. Parents have a special responsibility to teach, train, and make believers out of their children, believers of the consequences of crime. And then society must make the appropriate consequences happen. Consequences must fit the crime. All levels of government also have a critical responsibility, as do we, the voters.

The Appendices contain step-by-step instructions on making one's own self-help tapes. By using them, the reader can relax more easily and more deeply, and more easily modify the belief system. The reader may select from lists of positive affirmations to promote relaxation and wellness, build self-esteem, and to quit smoking. One Appendix includes a sample letter containing parents' rules for prospective child caretakers. Another includes a sample decision paper for assistance and support in otherwise stressful personal and workplace decisions.

Last Reminders - Honest

♦ RELAX. Seriously consider use of tapes. Appendices A-C.
♦ Remind yourself that you *understand others*.
♦ Remind yourself *what it is* that you understand.
♦ Do not expect understanding from others.
♦ This above all, to thine own self be true. (Shakespeare) No

185

rationalizing, no weak excuses, no blaming.

- No one knows enough to be pessimistic. (Robert Schuller)
- If you do not like what you are feeling, write about what you are feeling. If you overreact in any situation, lie back, try to relax, and ask yourself. "Where is this coming from?"
- Read your body. Tight muscles *anywhere* indicate emotional stress that needs resolution.
- You *will have ups and downs*. When down, remind yourself, "This too shall pass."
- Avoid procrastination even in little things.
- Avoid rationalizing. Be honest with yourself.
- Avoid gossip. It is in the same category as calling one names behind his back.
- Avoid criticizing until *you* are perfect.
- List your to-dos, prioritize them, and do them at first opportunity. Priorities may change as time passes. Reprioritize, daily if warranted.
- Let others retain their dignity, *especially* the very young.
- Teach others how to treat you.
- An unborn child feels physically, and hears.
- A newborn infant senses and remembers more than most adults realize.
- Children need training.
- *Report* suspected abuse of spouses, children, and the elderly.
- Accept circumstance as random and not directed at you.
- *God does not cause your problems*. He *does allow* them. He does not *take* anyone. He *invites* us. And all of this is so that we may have and make choices. Without choices, who and what are we?
- *Society* has a collective responsibility to help its members make the right choices.
- A manager makes decisions about which he feels the best, as do all of us.
- Child caretakers cannot know parents' expectations and requirements unless informed.
- Make assumptions *only if you must*.
- Be willing to be held accountable for what you say and do.

Be willing to be challenged.

- ♦ Con men play on the mark's *greed*. You have likely heard, "There's no free lunch."
- ♦ Silently forgive everyone who has *ever* offended you.
- ♦ Take care of number one, *you*.
- ♦ Especially for parents. What you have read may have caused you to think about how you acted around and reacted to your children. You may be wishing things had been different. Things *could not have been different.* In some situations, you did not know, and in others, you were emotionally driven and inhibited. Although you may feel regret, *you have no reason to feel any guilt.*

One CAN change for the better. Believe it, or believe it. *Pick one.* Either choice is OK.

Having tolerated the repetition, have you tired of repeatedly hearing politicians, public speakers, and panelists say, "Having said that, let me say ....?" Having written that, let me say, "This is the end." May God bless you in all that you do.

APPENDIX A
Relaxation Audio Tape

Important Message to the Reader

Nothing in this book is intended to interfere with any advice, care, or treatment by any physician, minister, or mental health care professional. This book contains material for informational and educational purposes only. It is not a substitute for professional care of any type. It is the responsibility of the reader to consult with his or her own health care professional to determine the appropriateness of making and using the self-help audio tapes as referenced in these Appendices. Appropriately use every possible source of help. Your mind is extremely powerful.

MAKE YOUR OWN RELAXATION TAPE.
FIRST, CAREFULLY READ THIS APPENDIX,
THEN PLAN YOUR TAPE.

The process may seem complicated, but it is not if you follow step-by-step instructions. Please read Appendices A-C before making your own tape.

- Appendix A may be used by itself as a relaxation procedure, or with affirmations in Appendices B and C.
- Affirmations and suggested visualizations may be selected from Appendix B (Build Self-esteem) or C (Wellness).
- If you make a tape only for relaxing, a 30-minute tape (15 minutes per side) is more than long enough. Consider including some positive affirmations.
- After playing this tape you will know what it means to relax. Do not let having to follow a procedure discourage you.

The more frequently you listen to affirmations, the sooner and more effectively will they become a part of your unconscious belief system.

Use your own voice, or request a friend to do the speaking. Omit or add whatever you deem inappropriate for your requirements. For your personal use, you may make a photocopy of the Copyrighted Appendices A-C for the purpose of marking and perhaps "cutting and pasting" for easier planning, reading, and recording of your selected affirmations.

If you choose to include affirmations from Appendices B or C, insert them as indicated at the word INSERT near the end of this Appendix A. You may want to repeat some of the selected affirmations to fill the tape.

The listed affirmations are written as though they are being spoken to you by another person. During childhood, your conscience, your beliefs, mostly came from others. I suggest you *first* use them as written. Later, you may wish to remake the tape using first person, i.e., I believe…I shall… My body… I am….

- The ellipses, series of dots, represent pauses, some longer than others.
- Observe the relative lengths. Use minimum 1-2 second intervals. If pauses are too long, your mind may drift to other thoughts.
- It may be helpful to make a short *trial* tape using only a few of the first relaxation suggestions.

1) Plan your tapes before starting to record.
2) Appendices A-C may be used individually or in any combination.
3) Leave enough space at the end of the tape to include the section at *** below, after the word, **Insert**.
4) Brief trial and error may be necessary, but your time will be well spent.
5) You may decide to use different affirmations on the reverse side.
6) If you want both sides identical, use a tape dubber to copy the first side of the first tape to a second tape.
7) Rewind the first tape.
8) Turn the second tape over.
9) Play first tape while recording second tape.

PLAN BEFORE YOU START RECORDING.

Text for recording relaxation affirmations is from an audio tape titled
RELAXATION. © copyright Howard Otterholt, Ph.D.

MAKING YOUR RECORDING

In your first recording of each type of tape, if you make minor mistakes that do not change the meanings, simply continue recording. You can make a more perfect tape after you have listened to it a few times.

Include the next paragraph (*). Start the tape in recording mode. Allow several seconds for tape leader to pass the recorder's read-write head.

Begin reading the following aloud: (Speak softly.)

* This tape is not to be used to avoid, replace, or defer the care, advice, or treatment by any physical or mental health care professional. This tape is not to be played near the driver of a moving vehicle or near anyone else whose full attention is required for any other reason. Make yourself as comfortable as you can in a chair, recliner, or lying down. You may wish to stop the tape while doing so......

Now lie back and rest..... Slowly close your eyes........ Take as deep a breath as you comfortably can and hold it briefly...... Let it all out and breathe easily............ Take another deep breath and hold it briefly....... Let it all out..... relax, and breathe easily............

As you relax, you will avoid any negative memories or emotions from the past. As you now deeply relax, all of your memories will be happy ones.....

Relax the muscles around your eyes............. Feel your forehead smoothen...... Feel it relax...... You have powerful muscles leading from your temples into your cheeks. Relax those muscles..... Feel them get longer....... Feel them get longer and longer as they relax......... Let that relaxed feeling move into your cheeks....... Feel the muscles in your cheeks relax..........

Let that relaxed feeling move into the muscles on the sides of your neck.......... Concentrate on them..... Let them relax........ Let that relaxed feeling move into those heavy muscles that lead from the back of your neck to each shoulder.... First, concentrate on the right side........ and now the left side........ Let that relaxed feeling move into the back of your neck........... imagine the relaxation is like a little wave moving slowly down the centerline of your spine...... It moves slowly down your spine all the way to the bottom...... Concentrate on the centerline of your spine as that wave of relaxation moves slowly downward....... Relax deeper - and deeper – and deeper.........

Again, feel the relaxed feeling around your eyes....... Let that relaxed feeling move into your cheeks..... Let the muscles in your throat relax......... The relaxed feeling moves into your right shoulder...... into your upper arm...... into your elbow..... into your forearm..... into your wrist..... into the palm of your hand..... into the back of your hand..... into your thumb - out to the tip of your thumb..... and into your fingers..... out to the tips of your fingers..... Feel the skin on the tips of your fingers - as you relax deeper - and deeper - and deeper...........

Now let that relaxed feeling move into your left shoulder - Feel it relax.......... That relaxed feeling moves into your upper arm..... into your elbow..... into your forearm..... into your wrist..... into the palm of your hand..... the back of your hand..... into your thumb - out to the tip of your thumb..... and into your fingers..... out to the tips of your fingers..... Feel the skin on the tips of your fingers - as you relax deeper - and deeper - and deeper...........

Relax the muscles in your throat...... Now let that relaxed feeling move into the muscles high up in your chest - feel the muscles relax......... Let that relaxed feeling move slowly downward into your stomach........... It surrounds your waist..... It moves into your hips..... That relaxed feeling moves downward into your right thigh - Feel it surround your thigh........ It moves toward your knee - and into your knee..... That relaxed feeling moves into the calf of your leg..... into your ankle..... It surrounds your heel..... It moves into the bottom of the arch..... the top of the arch..... and into the ball of your foot..... It moves into your toes..... out to the tips of your toes..... Feel the skin on the tips of your toes - as you relax deeper - and deeper - and deeper...........

Let that relaxed feeling start high up in your left thigh - feel it surround your thigh..... It moves toward your knee - and into the knee.... That relaxed feeling moves into the calf of your leg..... into the ankle..... It surrounds your heel..... It moves into the bottom of the arch..... the top of the arch..... and into the ball of your foot..... It moves into your toes..... out to the tips of your toes..... Feel the skin on the tips of your toes - as you relax deeper - and deeper - and deeper...........

Now let yourself be in a large walled patio with a swimming pool....... The water is so blue....... There are flowers planted next to the wall all around the patio........ In your mind see the blue water in the pool....... Imagine the reflection of the flowers on the other side of the pool...... Lie back and look up at the blue sky....... The beautiful blue is so relaxing...... As you relax, your whole body is being revitalized from the top of your head to the tips of your toes......... Relax deeper... and deeper... and deeper........

THIS IS THE END OF
THE RELAXATION SUGGESTIONS
If you wish to use the tape only for relaxation,

skip to * below.**

If you wish to use the tape to help you go to sleep at night, you may want to fill the remainder of the tape with selected affirmations and omit the section at **** below.

Appendix B contains affirmations to help build self-esteem.
Appendix C contains affirmations for wellness.

After each group of 6-9 affirmations insert the following:

"Relax now...... You are in your own peaceful place.......... Relax deeper - and deeper - and deeper....."

Insert affirmations here.
After inserting affirmations, continue below.

***

Feel how good it feels when you are relaxed..... Breathe easily and feel how good it feels just to breathe - just to be in this world when you are relaxed.......... (pause)

No one will ever be able to place you in this relaxed state unless you want them to do so........... You will never accidentally or unknowingly go into this relaxed state.......... When you desire to do so, you WILL be able to place yourself in this deep state of relaxation quickly and easily.........

(If you are to use this tape only to assist you in going to sleep, omit the following wakeup paragraph. Use a tape player that has automatic shutoff. Otherwise continue below.)

****

It is soon time to open your eyes.............. Feeling good all over...... Hold onto those good feelings...... At the count of five, open your eyes... one - two - three - four - five - eyes open - wide awake - wide awake.

Make a backup copy. Copy the backup to the second side of the first tape. This allows repeated playing without rewinding.

When using the completed tape, place yourself in a comfortable position so as to be able to relax for an extended period. Listen to the tape once daily, more if you have the time, until you can *will* yourself to relax.

APPENDIX B
Tape to Build Self-esteem

Text for recording the following affirmations is from a DocOtt audio tape titled BUILD SELF-ESTEEM © copyright Howard Otterholt, Ph.D.

IMPORTANT MESSAGE TO THE READER

Nothing in this book is intended to interfere with any advice, care, or treatment by any physician, minister, or mental health care professional. This book contains material for informational and educational purposes only. It is not a substitute for professional care of any type. It is the responsibility of the reader to consult with his or her own health care professional to determine the appropriateness of making and using the self-help audio tapes as referenced in these Appendices. Use every possible source of help. Your mind is extremely powerful.

Do not let the following procedure discourage you. The benefits may be more than you expected. Select any or all of the following affirmations. If you have strong doubts or negative feelings regarding a particular affirmation, it may be that you need it. Work at determining what it really is that bothers you and work on that.

1) If you choose to start with the relaxation method from Appendix A, record your selected affirmations on the tape location as indicated in Appendix A.
2) Follow this with affirmations selected from those below.
3) Repeat the selected affirmations until the tape is full.
4) Reverse the tape briefly.
5) Play tape and stop immediately at the end of the first affirmation you hear.
6) Next, record the eye-opening suggestion at the location marked (***) in Appendix A.

Pause 1-2 seconds between affirmations.

If the tape runs out while recording your list, you may be facing a bit of trial and error in adding the section at (***) in Appendix A. It will be well worth your effort. Rewind the tape a short distance. Play until you come to the end of a sentence and stop tape immediately. Next record the ending from Appendix A.

- To include the relaxing procedures, record the affirmations in Appendix A until you come to the asterisks (***).
- Then include selected affirmations from those below. Repeat selected affirmations until the tape is full.
- Rather than repeating the affirmations below, you may choose to mix wellness affirmations from Appendix C.
- If tape is full, reverse the tape briefly.
- Play briefly, stopping immediately at the end of the first affirmation you hear.
- Finally, record the wakeup suggestion in Appendix A (***). This may require trial and error.

MAKING YOUR RECORDING

If you have included relaxation affirmations, you have already recorded those affirmations and have stopped the tape and are ready to record affirmations from below.

If you want only to record self-esteem affirmations, **mark affirmations** to be included before starting your recorder. Wait a few seconds for the tape header to pass the read-write head and read selected affirmations below. Add your own if desired.

BEGINNING OF SELF-ESTEEM
AFFIRMATIONS
Pause 1-2 seconds between affirmations.
(Speak softly.)

We are all created equal.
You are just as good as anyone else. *Anyone.*
No one - no one is better than you.

Understand that everyone is driven by emotions.
Anyone who tries to put you down has an emotional problem.
Their *behavior* is driven by their *emotions.*

Recognize the childlike emotions in others.
No one can hurt you with childlike statements.
You understand their emotions - their childlike needs.

It is important to forgive them.
No one can hurt you with words. You recognize their emotions.
You can *do* whatever you decide to do.

Each of us is equal to everyone else.
Deep inside of you, you *know* you are an intelligent person.
You can accomplish *whatever* you reasonably want to *do*.

You do *not* need approval from others.
You only need your *own* approval.
You do *not* need to *compete* with others.

Compete only against your own standards, your own accomplishments.
Strive to improve in areas in which you want to improve.
Your *parents loved* you - even when they could *not show* it.
Your parents were *proud* of you - even when they could not show it.

Everyone is worthy of *feeling good*.
You are worthy of feeling good.

Deep down inside you *know* you are a *capable person*.
Put your *emotions to rest* through *understanding others.*
You can learn rapidly when your emotions are at rest.

If someone interrupts you when you are speaking, *that person has a problem*.
That person has an *emotional need*, a need to *prove* something.
You *understand* that person's emotional problem.

Look forward to change.
You can handle whatever comes your way.
You can be alone without feeling lonely.

Prioritize those things that need doing.
Do things that need doing - starting now.
Avoid fantasizing about the future.

Plan for the future.
Understand and forgive those who attempt to hurt you.
You forgive others. *Forgive yourself.*

No one can hurt you with *words* because you *understand others*.
Look at them with i*nteres*t.
You understand emotionally driven behavior.
.
You understand adult negative emotions from childhood.
It was not the *child's fault.*
It was *not* the *offender's* fault.

You forgive *everyone* that *ever offended* you.
If someone *ignores* you, *that person has a problem.*
You *know* you are a *good person.*

You are worthy of the *best*.
Be patient with yourself and others.
They cannot help behaving the way they do.

If others try to insult you or hurt you, *smile inside.*
You understand their childlike problems and needs.
You understand *others*. *Others* may not understand *you.*

Do *not expect understanding* from *others.*
Understand their *failure* to understand.
They had no one to teach them.

Avoid being judgmental.
Avoid telling others of their problems.
We are all born *equal*. We are worthy of health and happiness.

You *care about yourself.*
No one can *manipulate* you unless *you allow* it.
In a careful and caring way, let others know your desires.

Let others know how to treat you.
Teach them how to *treat* you.
Let others know the *limits* of what you will *tolerate*.

Smile while *talking* with others. It helps them to *feel good*.
Because you understand, you *forgive offenders*.
The negative words of *others* do not make *you* less than you *were*.

You understand their needs to put someone down.
You do not expect understanding from others.
You forgive them.

Negative words do *not make you less than you were*.
Positive words do not make you *more* than you were.
Money and *material* things do not make you more than you were.

You know *who and what you are* and what you *stand* for.
You have your *own values*.
There is *no place* in your life for *guilt*.

You instantly understand others' negative behavior.
Say to yourself several times, "*I believe in me*."
I can learn and do more and more every day.

Say to yourself several times:
God is on my side. I must be a winner.

If you included relaxation procedures,
after recording affirmations, go to (***) at end of App. A
to finish recording the tape.

APPENDIX C
Make a Wellness Tape

This Appendix contains affirmations for general wellness, and from DocOtt tapes titled, *NO! to Smoking Without Weight Gain*, and, *Christian Healing Power*,
both © copyrighted Howard Otterholt, Ph.D.

IMPORTANT MESSAGE TO THE READER

Nothing in this book is intended to interfere with any advice, care, or treatment by any physician, minister, or mental health care professional. This book contains material for informational and educational purposes only. It is not a substitute for professional care of any type. It is the responsibility of the reader to consult with his or her own health care professional to determine the appropriateness of making and using the self-help audio tapes as referenced in these Appendices. Use every possible source of help. Your mind is extremely powerful.

Select those affirmations from the list below that apply to your situation and to your objective. Plan your tape. Read Appendix A if you have not already done so.

1) In making your tape, you may choose to start with the relaxation method from Appendix A.
2) Record your selected affirmations on the tape location as indicated in Appendix A. Follow this with affirmations selected from those below.
3) Repeat the selected affirmations until the tape is full.
4) Reverse the tape briefly.
5) Play tape and stop immediately at the end of the first affirmation you hear.
6) Next, record the eye-opening suggestion at the location marked (***) in Appendix A.

Pause 1-2 seconds between affirmations.
If necessary, remake your tape until the pace and intervals

are right for you. Consider first making a brief trial recording using only a few affirmations. You can make a brief trial tape to check speed and ease in listening.

1) If the tape runs out while recording your list, you may be facing a bit of trial and error in adding the section at (***) in Appendix A. It will be well worth your effort.
2) Rewind the tape a short distance.
3) Play until you come to the end of a sentence and stop tape immediately.
4) Next record the ending from (***) Appendix A.

MAKING YOUR RECORDING

If you have included relaxation affirmations, you have already recorded those affirmations and have stopped the tape and are ready to record affirmations from below. You may choose to mix affirmations from other sections in this appendix.

If you want only to record Wellness affirmations, **mark affirmations** to be included before starting your recorder. Wait a few seconds for the tape header to pass the read-write head and read selected affirmations below. You may wish to include some of your own.

Beginning of
Appendix C Affirmations

Your *mind is powerful*.
Your *immune* system is powerful.
Your immune system produces the proper number of white blood cells *you need* to overcome illness.

Your white cells fight and overcome *any virus* or harmful bacteria.
You feel *healthier every day.*
You are a healthy *person.*

Imagine yourself striding up a long steep hill. You feel *great*.
Imagine yourself walking *rapidly*. It *feels good*.
You *are healthy*. You get healthier *every day*.

Feel your legs *driving hard*, *pushing* you *up the hill*.
You are working hard *striding up the hill.*
You are breathing *deeply*. It *feels good*.

Awake or asleep, your unconscious mind works at healing your body *every minute* of *every hour* of *every day*.
Your immune system is getting stronger *every moment* of *every day*.

Any injury heals *quickly*.
Your body regenerates *rapidly*.
You are *healthier* with *every beat* of your *heart*.

Imagine yourself walking *briskly*, breathing *deeply*.
You feel *good*.
You are healthier with *every breath you draw.*

Your unconscious mind is healing *every part of your body.*
It heals your *skin - muscles - tissues - tendons - every*
organ in your *body* - your *bones* - even the *marrow* in your bones.

You desire to be *well*.
You desire to get well *quickly*.
Your body *heals quickly.*

See a *continuous stream* of your *white blood cells* attacking *all harmful bacteria.*
Your body *heals quickly*.

Relax and let yourself *feel* the healing.
You understand others.
You *forgive*.

There is *no place* for anger in your life.
You *deserve* to be *healthy*.
Just relax and *let go*.

Your muscles get *stronger every day*.
Every organ in your body is being *revitalized*.
Know that you are healing *rapidly*.

You are *healing now.*

Are you a cancer victim? Many have rid themselves of dreaded cancer using relaxation and visualization.

You may choose to include the following affirmations along with selected affirmations from the above. Irrespective of your religious beliefs, if you are ill, it is important that you believe that you can and will get well. When Jesus was healing the blind, he said, "According to your faith it is given unto you." It is important that you strengthen your belief. I suggest you play the taped affirmations several times a day. In addition, every time you have even a small amount of spare time, use your imagination as suggested in the tape text. Use the imagery often, even when you have a few seconds to spare.

NO-TO-CANCER AFFIRMATIONS

Your unconscious mind controls your immune system.
You are producing *all the white cells you need* to *fight disease....*
Your *unconscious* works at this even while you *sleep*.

Your unconscious mind keeps busy healing you *every moment*, even while you are *sleeping*.
Your white cells *smash* the cancer cells into *harmless dust*.

Your *blood stream disposes* of the harmless dust.
Your body creates *all the white blood cells* needed to fight *any virus....*

Your white cells are *destroying* the cancer virus cells *right now*.

In your mind, *see* those white cells *attacking* the cancer virus cells.
In your mind, *see* that army of white cells *charging into the cancer* and attacking it.....

See an *endless column*, an *endless supply of white cells* attacking the cancer cells, *smashing* them into *dust*....

Imagine you have two flat plates of metal with handles similar to band cymbals. Smash those cancer cells between them. Again, and again....Harder.....

Slam those plates together with *all your might*. Smash *every cancer cell*.....
Destroy every cancer cell....

Imagine your white cells smashing the cancer cells into harmless microscopic *dust*.... The dust is being harmlessly drawn away by your blood stream.

Again *imagine* you *see* the cancer. Imagine you are *destroying it completely*. In your mind see the cancer *shrinking* until, *suddenly*, there is *nothing left* of the cancer.

(Do not use this suggestion if you are on *chemotherapy*.)
You *refuse to feed* the cancer. You are *starving* the cancer. It is *dying*. You see the cancer shrinking and shriveling to *nothingness. See it happen*.

The cancer is *shrinking*. It is shrinking like letting the air out of a *balloon*. See it getting smaller... and smaller... and smaller. It gets so small you can hardly see it.... It is like a small speck...
It has almost disappeared... *Suddenly* you cannot see it....

Imagine that you are climbing a long hill.
The scenery around you is beautiful. You are healthy and strong.

You feel the cool, clean air entering your lungs.

You *walk faster and faster*.... Imagine that you are *striding* up that hill.... *Feel* the muscles in your *legs*.... *Push hard* with your legs.... Imagine that you feel your leg muscles *driving* you up the hill.... You feel *better* with *every step you take.*

. You do *not need* the attention or pity from others. You are *free*. You are free to grow *healthier - every moment of every day*. You *refuse to accept illness*. You do *not benefit* in *any way* from illness.

Several times say to yourself as though you are shouting it, "*NO TO CANCER.*"..................

CHRISTIAN HEALING AFFIRMATIONS

(Book, chapter, and verse designations are intended for reference only but you may wish to include them on your tape. The Bible mentions image, imagery, and imagination in dozens of books. The power of visualization is clear. "Seeing is believing.")

Before his ascension, Jesus was given all power in heaven and on earth. (Matt 28:18)
Heavenly Father, we ask you now in the name of Jesus for help and guidance in our healing. Help us to set aside every negative thought and feeling that interferes with our faith.

You *WILL* be healed if you *believe*. Jesus *PROMISED*. (Matt 11:23)
Jesus did not lie.
Jesus said *whatever* we ask in *His name* will be *granted*. (John 14:14)

Jesus said he is with you *always*." (Matt 28:20)
When Jesus left, he left us with the Holy Spirit.

(John 14:16)
Jesus *told* you that He is *one with you*. (John 14:20)

Jesus is one with the Father. He is one with you.
This means *you* are one with the Father.
Jesus left the comforter. He left the *Holy Spirit* with you.

You are a part of the *most powerful healing team on Earth*.
You have the *mind of Christ*. (1 Cor 2:16)
You have the power to *heal your body*.

Jesus said that *if you believe* in him, you can do *greater things* than *he* did. (John 14:12)
The same Holy Spirit is in *you* that was in *Jesus*.
(Matt 10:20)

Jesus received *his* power *from God through the Holy Spirit.*
You have that same power if you have *faith,* if *you can believe.*
(Mark 9:23 Mark 11:23)

Jesus asked, "And why call ye me Lord, Lord, and do not as I say? (Luke 6:46)
He *is* your *Lord. Believe* him.
Jesus said all things are possible for you *if you believe*. (Mark 9:23)

Repeat *silently*, "I believe. I believe. Jesus, I *know* you did not lie......"
You have been given the *power to heal*. Jesus *told* you. (John 14:12)
Don't let anyone take away your confidence. (Heb 10:35)

Your *mind is* powerful. Belief in *God* makes your belief in yourself *more powerful.*
In healing the blind, Jesus said, "According to your *faith* it is *given* unto you." (Matt 9:29)

If you *believe* it, *whatever you say* will come *true*.

207

(Mark 11:23)
Say now, "I am *healed*. I *know* I am healed.
Jesus *did not lie*."…
Say now, "I believe *Jesus is my healer*.
He is *one with me*."…

You have the power to heal your skin, tissue, muscle, tendons, organs, and even your bones and the marrow in your bones. Say now, "Jesus, you *are* my *healer*."…

The belief in your mind is healing you now.
The brilliant white light of the love of God permeates every cell in your body.
You do your very best to *avoid offending others.*

You forgive *others* as God forgives *you*.
If you repent, you are forgiven for every offense you have ever committed.
You are *worthy* of *forgiveness*.
Guilty feelings have *no place* in your life.

No disease can withstand the Love of God.
God said, "Be still and know that I am God."
(Psalms 46:10)
Be *still* now. *Know* that *you have been given power by God.*

It is OK to *remind* God of his promises. (Isaiah 43:26)
Boldly claim your healing now. *Claim God's promise.*
(Heb 4:16)
Say to yourself now, "I say *NO! to illness*." I say *NO! to cancer*.…

Say now, "I am *healed*. I *know* I am healed."…
Say now, "I have *patience*. I *know it will happen. Jesus did not lie*."….

No one can *discourage* you. The *Word is truth*.
Now say silently to yourself several times, Jesus, you are my

208

healer."………

Now say silently to yourself several times, "*Thank* you, Jesus, for *healing* me."…….
Your patience will lead to *perfect health*. (James 1:4)
Paul told you to *run with patience* the race that is *set before you.*
(Heb 12:1)

ANTI-SMOKING AFFIRMATIONS
You may wish to repeat these affirmations
until the tape is nearly full.

You *care* about your *body*.
You *want* to *quit smoking.*
You want to quit because YOU want to quit,
not because someone *else* wants you to.

You want to quit. You *have* quit. *Do not light the next cigarette.*
You do *not need* to throw away your cigarettes.
Look at them with *contempt*.

Imagine you are holding a cigarette in your fingers.
Squeeze it… Crush it… Crumble it… See the tobacco falling…
You are not letting anything like *this* shorten your life.

Look at that pack of cigarettes with *contempt*.
You are *too important* to let them *control* you.
You are *not going to let that happen*.

You are in charge.
You *care* about your body.
You *care* about your *loved* ones.
Your *loved* ones want you to quit smoking.

Imagine being inside a mortuary.
Imagine seeing a young man lying in a casket...

209

He has a *hole* in his throat........
Before he died he had to breathe through a hole in his throat...
He believed smoking could never harm *him*.

As you leave, you walk through a room full of open caskets.
You look into them and see many that died too young....
They died from smoking.

Studies show that smoking accelerates death in *all* illnesses.
Look at them again.
One has surgery scars on his throat....
One has surgery scars on both cheeks *and* his throat....

Imagine seeing a middle aged woman with a plastic lower jaw....
She had smoked. *She* had believed it couldn't happen to *her*.
Imagine seeing her... Take a *good look*.....

She fed herself through that hole in her throat......
Imagine seeing a beautiful young woman holding an artificial
voice box to her throat......

Cancer *took her voice. She* had smoked.
She had believed it couldn't happen to *her*.
You are *proud* that you have quit smoking.

Someone else is proud of you.
You will not light the next cigarette.
You will not pick up or accept a lit cigarette.

AFFIRMATIONS FOR
MODERATION IN EATING

Imagine you are facing a full-length mirror....
Imagine you see yourself as you want to be....
This is your goal. You can attain it.

You will avoid *sweets*.
You will *eat proper foods*.
You *want* to take care of your *body*.

You *want* to eat *proper foods*.
You want to be at your *proper weight*.
It is for YOU, *not* for someone *else*.

Repeat silently:
Proper quantities of the right kinds of food are *delicious*, - *satisfying*, - and *nourishing*.

Rapidly repeat this to yourself several times,
"Proper quantities of the right kinds of food are delicious, satisfying, and nourishing."....…...(Pause 5-6 seconds.)

You *know* what kinds of food you should eat.
Be honest with yourself.
Avoid making excuses to eat improperly.

You will *avoid eating between meals.*
You have *no need* to eat between meals.
You will *avoid junk foods* and are *proud to do so*. *You* are in *charge*.

You will avoid junk drinks.
You will eat proper foods because *you* want to.
You are *too important* to allow yourself to be controlled by *food*.

As a tiny infant you were held close when you were fed.
You felt loved when you were being fed.
When you had something in your mouth you felt loved.

Some persons do not know *how* to demonstrate the love they *feel* for you.
Some others may love, but *only* to the *extent* they are *able* to love.
Understand that their problems *started* in *childhood*.

You will understand others. *Let yourself feel loved.*
You *feel loved without eating*.
Those who *loved* you, and who love you *now,*
may *not be able* to *demonstrate* love.

During childhood, *everyone else* was in control.
If someone *cannot* show their love, it is *not their fault.*
Understand and forgive.

You will eat *proper quantities* of food because you *want* to.
You will put *proper quantities* of food on your *plate*.
As you *finish eating* the food on your plate you *lose your appetite*.

Food will not control your life.
You are *too important* to let *that happen*.
Shakespeare said, "This above all,
to thine own self be true."

You will avoid *rationalizing*.
You will avoid *looking for excuses* to eat, drink, or smoke.
You are in charge of your life.

You *do* not need cigarettes, - tobacco, -
or drugs of any kind.
You are *too important* to let them *control* you.
You *do not need excessive* quantities of food.

Small quantities of the right kinds of food are delicious, -
satisfying, - and nourishing.
You do not need *junk foods* or *junk drinks*.
You are *proud* that you can leave them *alone*.

***Let your quest for health become an obsession. Use every
spare moment to use this visualization method. Seeing is***

believing. Your mind is powerful to do what you unconsciously believe. Play your tape(s) over and over.

APPENDIX D
Decision Paper

EXECUTIVE SUMMARY

The purpose of this summary is to save executive time. This of course cannot be written until the remainder of the paper is complete. Once a subordinate has developed a track record of complete, accurate and timely staff work, the executive will likely feel comfortable deciding after reading only the executive summary.

PROBLEM STATEMENT

Before proceeding with the paper, a clear understanding and statement of the problem is critical. Why is a decision necessary? What is to be gained? Who is affected? How will you know when and if the problem has been solved totally or in part?

BACKGROUND

Who else has had the problem, including other organizations if known? When? What did they do about it? Have you or your organization had it before? What happened then? Are there known historical expenditures? What has since happened that has a bearing on the problem or decision? What lessons were learned? What research has been done previously by you or others?

FACTS

What are the facts bearing on the decision? What are the Sources of those facts? How were they verified?

ANALYSIS

What are all of the possible solutions? What, if anything, is to be prevented, avoided, acquired, disposed of, or modified? List the pros and cons of each alternative. Document the reasoning, the thought processes, as much as is reasonable. How did you arrive at each as being a possible solution? What resources are required to implement? Time and money are the two basics, but give details. Are in-house skills available and what will be the effect on current assignments? What are the anticipated consequences deferring, or of implementing and of not implementing each alternative? Begin now as objectively as you can to rank alternatives in order of preference. If some are determined to be infeasible, why? Documentation of these may later save someone a lot of time.

ALTERNATIVES

Document all acceptable alternatives. Briefly restate pros and cons of each, including the likely consequences of implementing or not implementing each.

RECOMMENDATION

State your recommended alternative. Briefly again set down the pros and cons. Why do the pros overshadow the cons? Briefly state why you are rejecting the others. If it is a close call, do not allow yourself to over-explain. The reasons can be found in the sections above.

SUMMARY

If this is a very lengthy paper, write a summary. If not, only the executive summary is needed.

EXECUTIVE SUMMARY

Keep it brief. Attempt to contain it in one page only, two at the max. Write the executive summary and place at the front of the report prior to submission. Include: the problem statement; only the most significant facts; a sentence or two covering what key questions were considered in the analysis; your recommendation and the highest ranking alternative, and the *most significant* pros and cons of each.

APPENDIX E
Memo to a Child's Caretakers

NOTE TO PARENT(S): The memo below is only a suggestion for your consideration. You may choose to use portions, or none at all. By what ever means you choose, it is important to make your rules and expectations very clear to whoever it is with whom you entrust your children. If your parent, older child, or any other relative is to be the caretaker, make the same points to them. "Mom/Son/Sis, I'm composing a memo to give to the child caretakers we sometimes use. I'd like to know what you think of it. I'd appreciate any suggestions you might have."

MEMO

This memo is given to every person who takes care of our child. It is very direct, but we are not implying that you would ever commit any offense against any child.

You realize our child is precious to us. If abused sexually, emotionally or physically, he may be troubled for life, or worse. Please understand that our concern is based on our knowledge of what has happened to so very many children of all ages because parents have failed to use precautions in obtaining and managing the care of their children. We must give you our expectations.

Please understand we are not suggesting or implying that you would or even could offend our child. As parents, we feel a tremendous responsibility toward our child.. We hope you feel the same. You are substituting for us. We want you to be a caring caretaker.

RULES WHILE YOU ARE CARING FOR OUR CHILD

❑ Safety of our child is paramount. Safety requires careful watchfulness. Except for brief periods of necessity, please keep our child within your view at all times.
❑ Without our prior approval, please do not allow any guests in

our home.

- Never open the door for anyone unless you know with certainty who it is.
- Feed our child only as we have instructed you.
- Check on our child periodically even though he is asleep.
- When in our home or caring for our child in any location, we expect you to be completely sober and free of the effect of alcohol or street drugs.
- References will be checked.
- For well-known reasons, neither you nor your approved guests are allowed to possess or use tobacco, alcohol, drugs or any other abusive substance anywhere in our home or on our property.
- Never physically strike our child with your hand or by any other means.
- Never shake our child, even gently.
- Never run while holding or physically guiding our child in any manner.
- Never toss our child in the air in any direction.
- Never leave or allow our child within reach of objects small enough to be stuffed into the mouth.
- Never leave or allow our child within reach of sharp or hot objects, including beverages.
- Never leave or allow our child within reach of any toxic substances or medicines in any form or container including boxes, tubes, jugs, or bottles.
- Avoid touching our child's genitals except to the extent necessary to clean the child during changing of diapers.
- While changing diapers, avoid scolding or accusing our child of being messy or dirty.
- Avoid shouting at our child even in what you might call "fun." Shouting in anger at a child is emotional abuse.
- Use care never to expose yourself sexually in any manner to our child (even though an infant).
- Even though you are fully clothed, do your best to avoid having or allowing our child to touch your genital area or anyone else's with any part of the child's face, hands, or body.

- Avoid talking about anything sexual or fearful in any terms, either plainly or disguised.
- Avoid using profanity or coarse language in our home.
- Do not discuss religious issues with our child without first clearing it with us.
- If anything arises that presents a problem to you that you cannot solve, or if you begin to feel anger out of frustration, please contact us at the earliest opportunity. We'll come home immediately. We shall leave the written phone number under the telephone.
- Do not use our phone to call outside our calling area except in an emergency.
- Limit phone calls to ten minutes and use the phone infrequently. We may have a need to call you. If necessary you can call your party again after waiting a few minutes.

You may wish to add messages, or to delete or modify some of the above, or reject all of it. When I first wrote the instructions, I prefaced each one with "Please." I later decided to make them non-negotiable. You may choose otherwise.

About the Author

Dr. Otterholt's life experiences have been a mixed bag of the technical, academic, management, and therapeutic. He has a bachelor's degree in business technology, a master's degree in human behavior, a master's degree in psychological counseling, and a doctorate in clinical psychology.

He conducted original research for a master's thesis in the uncovering of inner conflict through the use of hypnosis. For his doctoral dissertation, he conducted original research in clinical hypnosis in the resolution of phobias including agoraphobia. Since 1972, he has conducted hypnotherapy with hundreds of clients, as many as half of them pro bono. He authored the book, *How to be Your Own Good Samaritan.*

During wartime, he was responsible for and taught U.S. Navy anti-aircraft fire-control equipment operation and maintenance. He serviced business accounting machines and computers, and managed the maintenance and use of each. He taught and managed the design of business information systems, and taught business and information systems management. He managed systems development and operations for business, local government, and as regional Director for the Federal Government. He was also Regional Director of Quality Assurance in the procurement of products from 200 manufacturers.

For the past six years he has worked as a part-time volunteer at a State Prison working with inmates on the resolution of anger and low self-esteem, and on the acceptance of circumstance. He works as a part-time business consultant and counselor.

www.ingramcontent.com/pod-product-compliance
Lightning Source LLC
Chambersburg PA
CBHW030429290526
45786CB00001B/202